... "an actor with the spark and intelligence to carry off just about anything."
—*The New York Times*

"One of the hardest working, most conscientious actors I've ever worked with."
—Director Ron Maxwell

"The only actor in America who can simultaneously talk, swig Jack Daniels, and put a Marlboro in his mouth."
—*The Village Voice*

"I have a wildness that people like."
—Dennis Quaid

HERE'S DENNIS QUAID—AS YOU'VE NEVER SEEN HIM BEFORE!

DENNIS QUAID

by Gail Birnbaum

A 2M Communications Ltd Production

ST. MARTIN'S PRESS/NEW YORK

Photo Research by Amanda Rubin

DENNIS QUAID

Copyright © 1988 by 2M Communications Ltd and Gail Birnbaum

Library of Congress Catalog Card Number: 88-061674

ISBN: 0-312-91247-1   Can. ISBN: 0-312-91249-8

Printed in the United States of America

First St. Martin's Press mass market edition/September 1988

10 9 8 7 6 5 4 3 2 1

DENNIS QUAID

• 1 •

THE FIRST THING YOU NOTICE ABOUT DENNIS QUAID is his grin—a sly, impish look in which his mouth becomes as big as all of Texas, his home state, and his eyes crinkle into mischievous slits.

Writers love it; it gives them a chance to inject a note of poetry into their prose. For example: "It plays around the edges of his mouth, threatening to materialize at the slightest provocation. When it finally spreads across his face, slow and easy, it transforms this basically good-looking-but-nothing-to-die-for guy into a major-league charmer, an irresistible seducer. . . . Tom Cruise might have borrowed it for *Top Gun*, but it belongs to Dennis Quaid: the smirk."

Or: "He grins. You know, the grin from the

1

movies. That sweet smile with the little feathers sticking to the edges . . . canary feathers."

It's the reason people have compared him to everyone from Jan-Michael Vincent to Harrison Ford. But the name that comes up most frequently next to Quaid's is that of the granddaddy of grins: Jack Nicholson.

It's not too farfetched a comparison; they've both perfected a look that can project either hypnotic animal magnetism or demonic possession, sometimes simultaneously. But Nicholson's grin is more maniacal, closer to a leer than a lure. There's something more benign about Quaid, something reassuring that lets you know that beneath that grin, beneath the heavy layers of charisma, there lurks a truly nice guy.

The fact that Quaid's irrepressible grin glows atop a body of quarterback perfection does not hurt one bit, either. Dennis Quaid is a hunk—albeit a charming, adorable, approachable one. That's why thirteen-year-old girls have his photos pasted around their mirrors, and why thirty-year-old women go to his movies and fantasize about a man like him.

Of course, it is nice to have nubile young fans going ga-ga over you, but to become a major player of Quaid's current status takes a lot more than just a pretty face or devastating smile. It takes, first of all, talent—which he has in abundance. And it requires being in the right place at the right time. In 1983, when Dennis had three films in release almost simultaneously, people were proclaiming it "the year of Quaid."

They were somewhat premature in their timing, though. It would take four more years—until 1987—for Quaid's talent and image to coalesce into one seamless, irresistible whole—the year when *People* magazine would hail him as one of the "25 Most Intriguing People of '87," *US* magazine would declare him "in" (as opposed to his brother Randy, whom they pronounced "out"), *GQ* would feature him on their cover, *Rolling Stone* would do a major spread on him, and numerous other publications would be scrambling to get this hot commodity onto their pages.

Why 1987? Of course, the fact that Quaid had three major feature films in the theaters that year—*Innerspace*, *The Big Easy*, and *Suspect*—had a lot to do with it. You've gotta be seen to be hot.

But there is also something about Quaid being the right man for troubled times, the perfect remedy for what ails us. Despite the remarkable diversity of roles he has played in his relatively short career, Quaid's enduring quality is that of a confident, easygoing, can-do kind of guy who consistently comes out on top. A sort of Oliver North without the ethical taint.

At a point when America was wringing its hands over everything from the Iran-*contra* affair to AIDS to the near-collapse of the stock

3

market, who needed a brooding, soul-searching, Hamlet clone in the theaters?

Quaid embodies a simpler hero, one who knows what he wants and has the brash charm to get it. He's the kind of guy who goes for the gusto, and with such relentless good humor that *Big Easy* director Jim McBride was moved to call him "one of the most astonishingly cheerful actors I've ever worked with."

That cheerfulness came in mighty handy during the twelve years of work that led to Dennis's recent "overnight success." Someone with a less genial attitude might not have persevered through a career marked almost as much by starring roles that slipped away (*Midnight Express, Urban Cowboy, An Officer and a Gentleman*) and parts in downright stinkers, as it has been by dream roles such as astronaut Gordon Cooper in *The Right Stuff*, the surly and confused Mike in *Breaking Away*, and the swaggeringly sexy cop Remy McSwain in *The Big Easy*.

It takes a special kind of person not only to hang in there while waiting for the big strikes, but to actually convince the audience that there's no place you'd rather be—nothing in the world you'd get a bigger kick out of—than acting in a movie like *Gorp* or *Tough Enough* or *Jaws 3-D*. The Quaid grin is obviously not just an exterior affectation; it comes from some profoundly positive place deep inside him.

It's no wonder that directors have found him

4

such a joy to work with. Peter Yates, who cast Quaid in *Breaking Away* and directed him more recently in *Suspect*, told the *Chicago Tribune*, "He'll give you anything and everything, anytime you want it. Dennis has this characteristic of credibility that makes him believable. He also works very, very hard."

Joseph Ruben, who last worked with Quaid on *Dreamscape*, stated to *Premiere* magazine, "I think Dennis has a genuine joy in being alive, and that translates into all of his roles. There's a glint in his eye that says, 'Do you want to play?' It can have a sexual undertone to a woman—or, to a man portraying a heavy, it says, 'Let's spar; let's see who's the baddest and boldest.'"

And Walter (*48 Hours*) Hill, who directed Quaid in one of his earliest films, *The Long Riders*, said, "I remember the first day I worked with Dennis. I knew he had the intensity, the talent, and the physicality to go all the way as a leading man."

It's been a bumpy ride at times, with some crises of confidence along the way. In 1983, when Quaid had already achieved some fame in films such as *Breaking Away*, *All Night Long*, and *Caveman*, he told *Playgirl*, "You see friends all around you who are banging their heads against the wall and you wonder why it didn't work out for them. You feel guilty, like you don't deserve it."

When he was in his twenties, Quaid told writer

Chris Chase in August of 1987, "I was carrying around a lot of emotional garbage, and I'm really glad I didn't make it back then. . . . Now I realize I deserve to be a success, and why not enjoy it? It's fun."

He has indeed gone all the way. He's earned the right to bask in the limelight, to graciously accept being picked by US magazine in its May 1988 readers' poll as one of the ten sexiest bachelors in the country, and to say with characteristic straightforwardness, "I like it, being a leading man. I like wearing suits and getting the girl."

▪ 2 ▪

IF YOU DON'T BELIEVE THAT DENNIS QUAID IS RED-hot, try finding an available copy of *The Big Easy* at a local video store. "It goes out as quickly as it comes in," the manager of one large urban store explained. "People wait by the return counter for it."

It is a lucky actor who finds, early enough in his career, a perfect role in a movie tailor-made to highlight his talents and capture the imaginations of viewers. Dennis Quaid is very lucky. *The Big Easy,* a romantic thriller about a series of drug-related murders involving corrupt members of the New Orleans police force, is that movie. And Remy McSwain, the mildly unscrupulous but charming New Orleans police lieutenant, is that role.

Sure, Quaid's been in lots of other movies, including some extraordinarily good ones. But none of them displayed to such advantage his multilevel appeal as a sex symbol, a man of action, and an enormously likable guy. He even gets to sing in *The Big Easy*, happily showing off another of his prodigious gifts.

Although many women would be altogether thrilled to end up in Dennis Quaid's arms, he has always been uncomfortable with being thought of as a hot number.

"I don't want to act with my chest," he said in an early interview. During the first years of his career, he often echoed that sentiment. When Earl Wilson mentioned his beefcake persona, Quaid groaned, "I don't want it. A face on a candy wrapper today, forgotten tomorrow."

But since he has become more successful, Quaid—almost like a stunning woman who's finally proved she also has brains so she can relax about her beauty—has mellowed on the pretty-boy issue. He has come to accept, and even relish, his image as a sexy guy.

When a reporter pointed out that he was definitively established as a "heartthrob," Quaid just grinned his devastating grin and said, "Yes, I've heard that. But it's not like I wake up in the morning and go, 'Oh, you heartthrob, you! How are you today? Go out and throb some hearts!"

The hard-earned, still somewhat uneasy peace Quaid has made with himself comes across loud and clear in *The Big Easy*. He's so alluring because he exudes the self-confidence of a sexy guy, yet he avoids the arrogance of someone who's always banked on that quality. Remy McSwain/Dennis Quaid wants to be liked for himself, too.

The Big Easy wasn't always called *The Big Easy*. That title, the native slang name for New Orleans, was Quaid's contribution, something he picked up while jamming with a band at a Cajun club. Back when Jim McBride was hired by a small, independent company called Kings Road Entertainment to direct the project, the script was called *Nothing But the Truth*.

McBride's only Hollywood directing credit to date was a 1983 remake of the classic Jean-Luc Godard film, *Breathless*, starring Richard Gere in the Jean-Paul Belmondo role of a reckless petty criminal and newcomer Valerie Kaprisky in the part of his lover, previously played by Jean Seberg.

McBride's *Breathless* was considered a commercial washout, and Hollywood types weren't exactly breaking down his door to offer him more directing work. Eventually, though, his agent sent him the script for *The Big Easy*, penned by Dan (*Beverly Hills Cop*) Petrie Jr.

McBride's reaction was tepid; he told the *Chicago Tribune* that he thought "it was a story about police corruption set on fairly familiar ground." On the other hand, he said frankly, "I needed the job. I don't get to make movies too often." But he thought the script did have potential once some major changes were made.

Instead of setting the story in Chicago, as the original script had it, McBride wanted it relocated to New Orleans. Making a movie about police corruption in Chicago was almost redundant, too "predictable and boring ... to me, the question of taking money under the table in New Orleans is a much more ambiguous and much more interesting question than doing the same in Chicago," he told *American Film*. "The whole way things work down there is oriented around family and personal relationships."

McBride also objected to the focus of the original script, which was a complicated murder plot. He suggested that the love story in the background become the featured element, and that the characters be expanded from a stereotypical "bad guy meets a good woman and gets converted" to a much more subtle, complex interaction.

McBride's conception, as it got played out, was of two flawed people who fall in love and learn from each other. Quaid's police lieutenant Remy McSwain is flawed by his casual attitude toward questions of ethics; he thinks the practice of policemen extorting money from local merchants for a "widows and orphans" fund, for instance, is perfectly acceptable. That's just the way it's done down in the Big Easy.

10

But Remy is also a sweet guy with strong and loyal feelings for his family and friends. And he has his own not-altogether-unreasonable set of priorities based on the New Orleans code of behavior and living; he knows how to squeeze the joy out of life and generously spread it around to others.

On the other side of the coin is assistant district attorney and newcomer to New Orleans Anne Osborne (Ellen Barkin)—repressed, rigid, so obsessed with her mission to root out corruption among the New Orleans cops that she's unable to see that life is not always clearly defined in black and white.

What shakes them both up is a string of murders linked to drug-running activities among some of Remy's colleagues in the police department. What started out as nickel-and-dime extortion ends in murderous corruption. The world, it turned out, wasn't quite as nice and easy as Remy had thought; neither, however, was the path of corruption as clear-cut as Anne had figured it. In the end, they do learn from each other, not in the "bad guy meets a good woman and gets converted" kind of way, but in a much more subtle, profound manner.

McBride said that he felt "the story of these two people and their relationship was the most important thing about the movie. One of the first things we did was hire Dennis Quaid to play the lead. We all agreed on that. And, for me, as soon as we saw Ellen Barkin, she was

11

the one who seemed right for the part: It was clear that there was this kind of chemistry between Dennis and Ellen.''

The folks at Kings Road Entertainment weren't so sure about Barkin—a terrific, offbeat actress originally from the Bronx who has stood out in such roles as the young wife in Diner, Robert Duvall's daughter in Tender Mercies, JoBeth Williams's sister in Desert Bloom, and Timothy Hutton's wife in Daniel. They "wanted to hire some pretty young thing," Quaid related. But Barkin won out because of McBride's insistence and Quaid's threat to quit otherwise.

"And I threatened to quit later because they wanted to cut the sex out of the film, and it's a love story," Quaid recalled. Barkin performed her role perfectly and it was the electrical charge between her character and Quaid's that made the movie sizzle with some of the most erotic scenes this side of Last Tango in Paris, minus the overt sex, of course.

Who wouldn't melt back into the pillow as the uptight Barkin did when Quaid seductively crooned his favorite line, this time delivered like a soul kiss: "Just relax, darlin', this is the Big Easy. Folks have a certain way of doin' things down here." When he persists with this seduction, Barkin again tries to resist. "Stop that," she says halfheartedly. "Stop what?" he caresses. "That," she tries to explain. "What, that? Or that."

As People magazine exclaimed, "Oooowee,

here is one scorchingly sexy movie ... it's hard to unglue your eyes from Quaid and Barkin, two actors in starmaking performances. Their love scenes are hotter than anything in K-Paul's Louisiana kitchen. Rate this movie W for Whew!"

Professionals though the actors are, it seems that the excitement seen on the screen wasn't just method acting. "Dennis is a very sexy guy," Barkin stated in *Rolling Stone*. "That love scene was as fun as it looked."

Nearly as sexy as the actors in this inimitable love scene is the music accompanying it, a bewitching ballad called "Closer to You." Dennis wrote that song himself on the set one day, and he introduced it through the back door during the filming of another scene, one in which Barkin was escorted against her will to a barbecue Quaid and his family were having at his mother's home. While the cameras were rolling on a close-up on Barkin, Quaid was supposed to stand near the camera and sing to her to help her portray the right emotion. Instead of singing the designated number, however, Quaid snuck in his own composition. "It brought a tear to Ellen's eye—it was very emotional," recalled McBride.

Taking the initiative like that was typical of the way Quaid works. Before shooting on *The Big Easy* began, he spent three weeks in New Orleans preparing for his role of Remy McSwain by running around with local homicide cops every day to learn their way of walking, talking, and dealing with each other. "By the time we started shooting," McBride said, "he *was* this guy."

The funky Cajun accent Quaid used to play Remy was a departure for him because he has said he usually thinks playing an accent is a trick. Here, though, he realized that the voice was as essential to The Big Easy as its music, a rousing score of Cajun zydeco and rhythm-and-blues sounds.

But don't blame Quaid for portraying Remy as a fast-talking cop. It was McBride who actually urged his actors to speed up their delivery to compensate for the fact that the script was 138 pages long, compared to the standard 115 or 120 pages (the usual estimate is that one page of script translates to one minute onscreen). He even called the cast together for a screening of Howard Hawks's His Girl Friday—"which has the fastest talking in movie history"—to give them an idea of the pace he wanted.

"I told them, 'This is the way we have to play this movie,'" McBride explained. "They all got the point immediately. It became a kind of competition to see how fast we could do something and still keep the integrity of the emotional changes. It . . . gave shape to a lot of scenes that were amorphous on the page."

Yet the completed $6.5 million production of The Big Easy, good as it was, could not find any takers among the major film distributors; it wasn't a "high concept" flick that could easily be marketed with catchy one-line phrases. So by February of 1987, the film was slated for a modest distribution by a small independent company—almost a guarantee of instant obscurity.

Fortunately for all involved, David Puttnam, the maverick new head of Columbia Pictures at the time, waltzed in during the final moments of the closing act. He was attending the United States Film Festival in Park City, Utah, and sat directly in front of Quaid and McBride during the screening of *The Big Easy*. When he heard the audience's applause at the end, Puttnam turned around and said, "I want to buy it." Yes, Virginia, there is a Santa Claus.

With a major studio behind it, *The Big Easy* received the launching it deserved, and a number of influential reviewers were enchanted by it. *New York* magazine's David Denby said it was "greatly entertaining—a comedy-thriller that is also serious about romance and morals in the stirring way the old Tracy-Hepburn movies were. . . . I had a terrific time and went back to see it again." Quaid, added Denby, "gives a smashing performance . . . the wide grin practically says, 'C'mon, you like me, so why fight it?' "

Roger Ebert of the *Chicago Sun-Times* awarded *The Big Easy* four stars, calling it "one of the richest American films of the year. . . . I believe the plot of this movie is only an excuse for its real strength, the creation of a group of characters so interesting, so complicated, and so original that they make a lot of other movie people look like painting by numbers."

The positive reviews were translated into healthy earnings at the box office. On September 11, 1987, *The Wall Street Journal* reported, "For those who haven't been paying attention, *The Big Easy* has been the end-of-the-summer sleeper that's one of the sexiest, funkiest thrillers to come along in a long while. After a successful limited run, Columbia Pictures opened the film nationally two weeks ago. It took in more than $9 million its first eleven days." And that was on the heels of the earlier overseas distribution that had established *The Big Easy* as a big hit in European cultural bastions such as Paris.

With the success of *The Big Easy*, Dennis Quaid had arrived in a big way.

▪ 3 ▪

"A PERSON HAS TO REMEMBER WHERE HE COMES from and not believe his own publicity," Dennis Quaid once prescribed as the antidote to Hollywood schizophrenia. The Texas drawl may have softened, but he has no doubts about his roots. "I guess I'll always be a Texan, no matter where I am."

What more appropriate place for an all-American boy with big dreams to hail from than Houston, Texas? Until recently, this Sunbelt boomtown was the fastest-growing urban center in the United States, exploding from the oil frenzy below ground and the space race high above it (thanks to the Johnson Space Center). With the boom came other symbols of striving: major art and cultural institutions and, not least of all, the Houston Astrodome.

Quaid's Texas origins go back to his pioneering grandfather, who pushed to the west from Tennessee in a covered wagon in 1903. Though Dennis himself would eventually push even further west—to the more promising acting shores of Hollywood—his boyhood was steeped in country-and-western legends.

"He has been nourished and enriched by the music of Hank Williams, Ernest Tubbs, and Willie Nelson," stated a publicity release for one of his early movies, *The Night the Lights Went Out in Georgia*. "Cowboy Jack Clemens, who was a front man for Elvis and has produced many of Johnny Cash's recordings, is Dennis Quaid's own personal hero." Gene Autry was his second cousin.

Born on April 9, 1954, Quaid remembered his early youth as idyllic, a chapter straight out of Huckleberry Finn. "I had one of the great American boyhoods of all time," he once said. "I lived on Maple Street, for God's sake . . . we did all those American-kid things of growing up. You're playing baseball or you're throwing rocks, playing guns or playing war, and you have a contest to see who can die the best death. Or sitting out there on the grass, suckin' on reeds and tellin' dirty jokes when your parents are in the house. . . ."

Quaid's home was always lively with entertainment, courtesy of his electrician-cum-frustrated-actor father, Buddy, who bore a strong resemblance to actor Dana Andrews and often entertained his sons by tap dancing around the house or singing like Bing Crosby or Dean Martin.

Quaid senior, who used to point out actors he admired to his sons, even went so far as to have some screen tests himself. But it was bad timing: World War II was unavoidable, and he ended up donning fatigues and shipping out before any roles materialized.

It could be chalked up to coincidence if only one of the Quaid offspring had been bitten by the elder Quaid's acting bug. But the fact that both Randy and Dennis became committed to acting careers as early as high school indicates some overwhelming combination of inherited talent plus a drive to fulfill their father's acting dreams (unless you believe the quip both brothers have repeated ad infinitum over the years—that they got into drama in high school because it was taught in the only air-conditioned room in their school).

Not that Mr. Quaid was overly enthusiastic about his sons' aspirations at first. "He was set against us acting in high school," Randy has said. "He thought it would keep us from our homework." But his hesitation had softened by the time he saw Randy emoting up on the big screen in *The Last Detail* in 1974. "That's my son up there!" Buddy Quaid beamed.

When Dennis was thirteen, the bubble of his blissful childhood burst wide open. His father and his mother, Rita, who had ventured from

homemaking into real estate a few years earlier, were divorced. About a year later, older
brother Randy went out on his own. In time,
Dennis's father would remarry and have two
more children, another boy and a girl. But for
the moment, Dennis was left to puzzle out the
mysteries of adolescence by himself.

It was not a happy experience. "I was very
frightened as a kid," he has said. "I was miser-
able from about eleven to nineteen." No longer
wrapped up in the blissful cocoon of childhood, he hadn't yet matured into his current,
self-assured adulthood. He has described his
younger self to *People* magazine as "a goonball—
too small and skinny to make the football team.
I wanted to be a big hit with [girls], but I was
too shy."

Nor did he have the rich-kid luxury of end-
less money and leisure time to use to get himself into trouble. Quaid's teenage years were
marked by a succession of part-time and summer jobs—all of which, in one way or another,
called for some acting skills. It was probably
the best apprenticeship a kid with aspirations
of a show-biz career could have dreamed of.

There was the job as a clown at Houston's
AstroWorld amusement park, for instance.
("Now *that's* masochistic," he said in an interview.) Dennis remembered that the kids were
particularly cruel to clowns because they wanted
to prove they weren't real. "Children hate
clowns, man," Quaid said. "They think because

you've painted on a face it gives them full license to take out their frustrations on you. They'll kick you, they'll do anything." It must have taken a hell of an acting job for Quaid to restrain himself when he overheard a father tell his son, "Look, kick the clown. He'll laugh."

Then there was a job as a door-to-door encyclopedia salesman. There was clearly no love lost there when Quaid described it as "the worst job I ever had. It was like, 'Hi, mind if I come into your house and screw you out of seven hundred and fifty dollars and give you a genuine simulated naugahyde bookcase to go with it?' "

He was a little more charitable when recalling his stint as a Fuller brush man—a job he enjoyed because he felt he was a welcome sight to lonely little old ladies. Probably more to satisfy the ham in himself than the salesman, young Dennis perfected an English accent to go along with his brush pitches. Happily, he discovered that it commanded the attention, and opened the purse strings, of suburban Houstonites.

Dennis also did construction work for a time. Here, too, he remembered the job more for its dramatic interpersonal clashes than the work itself. "The guys wanted to fight me a lot," he explained, "because I was young and I had everything ahead of me, and I hadn't made the mistakes they had."

Most directly related to Quaid's acting bug

was his short—very short—run as a stand-up comic at a strip joint. As soon as his mother found out about his appearances at this unsavory venue, she put a stop to them. But not before Dennis was able to witness his first strip tease: an elaborate low-Shakespearean affair in which a girl undressed to the theme from the movie version of *Romeo and Juliet*.

He also had a more respectable stand-up gig at Houston's Tidelands Hotel, where he did impressions of Lyndon Johnson, Richard Nixon, and W.C. Fields and parodied such ads in comic books as "X-ray Glasses!" and "Learn Karate at Home."

After graduating from Houston's Bellaire High School, Dennis followed his brother Randy's lead and entered the drama department of the University of Houston. It's not a place one would automatically associate with top-flight acting talent, but in fact has turned out an impressive array of performing artists in recent years. Among the university drama department's better-known students, in addition to the Quaid brothers, is Tony Award-winner Tommy Tune—a multitalented choreographer/dancer/director who starred in the plays *The Best Little Whorehouse in Texas* and *Nine*, and was a smash hit co-starring with Twiggy on Broadway in *My One and Only*.

In a 1984 interview with the *Houston Post*, Sidney Berger, chairman of the drama department at the University of Houston, attributed his students' professional success to the department's "preprofessional approach" to acting. "A lot of schools will not allow their students to perform at all for the first two years," he said. "Unlike some university programs, we're not snobbish—we don't think we have the 'truth' about theater. We want our students to participate in theater out in the community and learn from the professionals at all levels."

That philosophy obviously influenced Randy Quaid. While still a college drama student, he was tapped by a Houston casting director to play the part of the hick named Lester Marlow (Cybill Shepherd's escort to the graduation party) in Peter Bogdanovich's smash hit, *The Last Picture Show*.

With such a remarkable film debut, Randy was soon landing an impressive string of parts. In 1974, he received an Academy Award nomination as Best Supporting Actor for his brilliant performance as a court-martialed sailor being escorted to the Navy brig by Jack Nicholson in *The Last Detail*.

Meanwhile, Dennis was working hard at the University of Houston to hone his own acting talents. Cecil Pickett, one of Dennis's professors and father of another successful drama department graduate, Cindy (*Ferris Bueller's Day Off*) Pickett, said that both Quaid brothers were easy to spot. "Randy and Dennis were undeniable. They both had such an abundance of talent that anyone could have seen it. They were electrifying."

Of Dennis, Pickett said, "He was probably one of the most tenacious students I ever had. I won't say he was hungry, because that sounds so trite. But . . . if he wasn't in a major production, he would be in a workshop of some sort."

It was a time for Dennis to experiment with different acting styles—trying on the personas of his favorite actors: James Dean, Marlon Brando, Montgomery Clift. College, he said, was "a good place to fall flat on your face and not pay the consequences."

Eventually, of course, Dennis settled into his own particularly Quaidian style. Pickett has likened the now-successful Dennis to Gary Cooper; just as Cooper could go through a string of roles yet still project a distinctive essence, so "you'll never see the image of Dennis totally disappear."

Diligent as he was in college, the impact of his brother Randy's virtual overnight success in the real world—the Hollywood world—was not lost on Dennis. Most important, as Dennis has put it, was the fact that Randy "made me see that you *can* work—you *can* make a living at this. It wasn't just a fairy tale."

The weeks that Dennis spent with Randy on location in Montana while Randy was filming *The Missouri Breaks* also reinforced his determination to make it as an actor. He had a ball, hanging out with Randy and his costars Marlon Brando and Jack Nicholson, and even coaching Brando on the mandolin.

"Brando was my idol, but you get over that adulation stage quickly," said Dennis. "You realize he's just a human being—that he goes to the bathroom like everyone else. It emphasized the importance of being a serious actor, not just a 'star.' "

More than halfway through his studies at the University of Houston, Dennis packed his bags and set out on the "yellow brick road" to Hollywood.

Dennis's impatient yearning for success was not hampered by long bouts of self-doubt. If youthful cockiness is a prerequisite for movie stardom, he was certainly destined for stellar heights.

"I really didn't think twice about it," he told the *Houston Post* regarding his departure for Hollywood a few days before his twenty-first birthday, with no prospects in sight. "I knew there were thirty thousand actors in the Screen Actors Guild, and that only one percent of them get jobs. I just figured I was in the one percent."

• 4 •

AND SO HE WAS—ONLY NOT RIGHT AWAY. THERE IS some small justice in the fact that even a guy like Dennis Quaid, to whom everything seemed to come so naturally, had to pay his dues when he arrived in Hollywood.

He left Houston with $1,000 he had saved from his various odd jobs, a $50-a-week unemployment insurance stipend, and two friends who also wanted to break into acting. Together they rented a tiny apartment in West Hollywood, rotating between sleeping on the bed, the couch, and the floor. The size of the kitchen was irrelevant because they lived on peanut-butter-and-jelly sandwiches and sardines.

Perhaps Dennis thought he'd have an easier go of it because big brother Randy had already been in Hollywood for several years. But Randy offered little practical assistance. Dennis once joked that when he got to town, Randy greeted him at the door with a blunt "Don't expect any help from me."

He also said that when he first tried to break into show business, Randy "wanted me to change my name so he would be the only Quaid." More seriously, Dennis recalled that Randy "helped me out quite a bit psychologically but he couldn't help me get an agent or anything."

But Dennis was unswervingly determined to make it as an actor, even if he had to do it on his own. "I made up my mind before I left Houston I would never work at anything other than as an actor, because a lot of people were telling me at the time to study something else to fall back on. Well, if you're going to do it, you're going to do it, and if you have something else to fall back on, you just might not do it," he said determinedly.

Though he didn't resort to other employment, Quaid also did not sit around waiting for acting work to find him. While his two buddies from Texas gave up and went home, Dennis approached the task of getting acting jobs with the same cheerful resolve he has since become known for on film sets.

Using his meager nest egg, he enrolled in an acting class, auditioned for the Actors Studio, and had the obligatory portraits taken, which he sent around to dozens of agents and casting directors. Most refused to see him, but finally, one casting director took a liking to him and introduced him to an agent who sent him on a round of auditions.

Quaid's biographical material has often stated that his first part was a small walk-on in a bizarre, early Jonathan Demme movie called *Crazy Mama*, starring Cloris Leachman. But a careful examination of the film on video shows no sign of Dennis. Most likely he was left sprawled on the cutting-room floor.

It makes for a much better story that Quaid finally landed his first real movie role exactly a year to the day after he drove into Hollywood. The film was called *September 30, 1955*, and it was about the devastating effect James Dean's death had on a group of college students in a small Arkansas town. And that film almost didn't even get released!

Janet Maslin of *The New York Times* documented the behind-the-scenes horror story: "*September 30, 1955*" [which was renamed from the original 9/30/55 because audiences didn't immediately recognize the numerals as a date] "would seem to have all the earmarks of a winner...." she wrote on January 23, 1978. "But Universal has had a terrible time marketing the movie, which has been ready for almost a year. The studio is now in its fifth ad campaign, and no end is in sight. No New York opening is in sight yet, either."

The problem, explained Maslin, was that "the spirit of the movie is complicated and hard to convey in the space of a slogan or on a poster, so it has been test-marketed a number of times, in order to try out various approaches."

Finally opening in New York in April 1978, *September 30, 1955* is largely an autobiographical slice-of-life from its director, James Bridges. The title stands for the date James Dean died so horribly in a car crash.

When the movie's central character, Jimmy J., played by Richard (*The Waltons*) Thomas, hears the news, he freaks out; James Dean, the lonely, neglected, misunderstood star of *Rebel Without a Cause* and *East of Eden*, was his idol, the one person in the world who could express Jimmy J.'s own adolescent yearnings and frustrations.

Jimmy J.'s circle of friends is comprised of "a group of highly talented but as yet unknown actors and actresses, chosen from hundreds throughout the United States," according to the film's production notes. They include Dennis Quaid as Frank, a "fun-oriented fraternity boy," as well as Thomas Hulce as Hanley and Dennis Christopher as Eugene.

Some of them understand Jimmy J.'s obsession with Dean, but Frank is one of those who ridicule the big fuss he's making over "a neurotic movie star," and go on with their lives of frat parties and homecoming parades.

Sounds like a pretty straightforward role for

Quaid, but his debut in the major leagues made him understandably nervous. "I had done a couple of long shots that day and when they brought the camera in for a close-up I was intimidated," he recalled. "All of a sudden, I had this big eye watching me. It took me about seven takes. Finally I asked Jim Bridges, the director, if I could have a second and I went off and yelled as loud as I could to get all the nervous tension out of me."

The producers worked hard to give *September 30, 1955* a realistic "small-town America in the fifties" look. It was shot in twenty-four days on location around Conway, Arkansas—condescendingly described in the production notes as "a typical all-American rural community, blessed with three colleges, a handful of churches, many dairy farms, and residents whose only contact with celebrities is through their local movie theater and their TV sets." Then the much-acclaimed cinematographer Gordon Willis shot the film in deliberately muted colors to capture the snapshot-like quality of fifties' films.

The film's production notes end on a high note: "According to Bridges, *September 30, 1955* was conceived as pure entertainment. But ultimately, he says, 'If people want to find a message, that's up to them and okay with me.'"

Several years later, however, Bridges seemed to try to distance himself from his film, saying, "I am embarrassed now by my worship [of

31

Dean]. If I had an actor in one of my films who performed like Dean, I would throw him off the set."

The critical reception of September 30, 1955 was mixed. The New York Times's Janet Maslin loved it, calling it a "superlative sleeper" and praising it with such lines as, "It's an exceptionally graceful movie, carefully structured, yet full of surprises, with a finely wrought sense of place that in no way interferes with its wider meaning."

Other reviewers were less charitable. Judith Crist, then of the New York Post, said it was "a very mawkish and incredibly dumb PG-rated [movie] . . . approaching a peculiarly complex subject in particularly simpleminded terms."

Eventually, the prophetic words of Janet Maslin—"the film may not be widely distributed anywhere, turning into one of those instant classics nobody ever sees"—came true.

The movie has developed something of a cult status, occasionally turning up at college film festivals on the anniversary of James Dean's death. But don't expect to find it in the local video store. Or at least not until Dennis Quaid achieves the kind of superstar status where everything he's ever breathed in is released.

Luckily, September 30, 1955's sad fate did no lasting harm to any careers. Jim Bridges went on to direct a number of illustrious projects, including The China Syndrome and Urban Cowboy. Gordon Willis became Woody

Allen's preferred cinematographer. Dennis Christopher went on to star in *Breaking Away*, and Thomas Hulce in *Amadeus* and *Dominick and Eugene*.

And Dennis Quaid continued getting the stepping-stone roles on the path toward leading-man stardom. If that road had more detours than he might have preferred, he realized the hidden advantages in retrospect.

In 1983 he said, "Instead of getting one big role early in my career, and then having the pressure of that, I'm glad I got to play supporting parts which were characters, and really get an education in film, rather than just having the whole film on your shoulders to begin with."

So the education of Dennis continued.

Because of the delayed release of *September 30, 1955*, Quaid actually made his onscreen debut in the film *I Never Promised You a Rose Garden*. It is the harrowing tale of a sixteen-year-old schizophrenic girl's struggle to regain her sanity in a mental hospital, based on a 1964 bestselling autobiographical novel of the same title.

Rose Garden, like *September 30, 1955*, was plagued by off-the-set problems. Already in 1970, *The New York Times* was reporting that the project was scheduled to go into production under Czech director Jan Kadar, starring Liza Minnelli and Estelle Parsons. And before that, said the *Times*, Natalie Wood and Sydney

33

Pollack had joined in an aborted effort to bring the book to the big screen.

Six years later, in June of 1976, *Variety* reported that *Rose Garden* was planned to "roll in late summer, with Peter Medak directing a cast hopefully headed by Isabelle Adjani (young French actress who won an Oscar nomination for . . . *The Story of Adele H.*)." When it finally was filmed, *Rose Garden*, released in July of 1977, was helmed by director Anthony Page and starred Kathleen Quinlan and Bibi Andersson.

Quaid pops up at the very end, as the bare-chested pitcher in a local softball game. He's a sort of benign macho bully who gibes at Kathleen Quinlan when she asks if she can hit a ball, "So, little Josephine DiMaggio wants to be in the big leagues, huh? I want you to look out for this one 'cause it's gonna breeze right by you, little girl."

But bare-chested is perhaps a key word, since it's become something of a trademark for Dennis Quaid. It's amazing, over the years, how many excuses directors have found for Quaid to take off his shirt, whether he's going for a dunk in the swimming hole in *Breaking Away*, romping with dinosaurs in *Caveman*, or washing his car in *All Night Long*. *Rose Garden* is notable as the place where fans received their first peek at those impressive abdominal muscles, often referred to as "abs."

Reviewers tiptoed shyly around this difficult

but well-intentioned story. The *Time* critic, for instance, waffled: "It leaves one feeling respectful but not deeply impressed or moved."

Reviewers had no such trouble assessing Quaid's next picture. "*Our Winning Season*," the *Variety* critic wrote, "is a lackluster little film that goes nowhere with a story of a young athlete struggling against life's hard knocks. Despite a fresh young cast . . . outlook seems confined to the ozoner circuit, where the audience doesn't much care what's happening on the screen."

As part of the young team of actors, Dennis Quaid played the screwy pal of high school track star Scott Jacoby. It might not sound like much of a role, but it gave *Variety* a chance to say one of the few nice things in its review: "Acting kudos go to Dennis Quaid as Jacoby's manic buddy. In one of the few nonstereotyped pot-smoking scenes of recent films, Quaid is outstanding."

• 5 •

PROFESSIONALLY, DENNIS QUAID SEGUED NEATLY from what could have been a career setback with *Our Winning Season* into a plum role in the hugely successful *Breaking Away*. And personally, he began his own winning season—a romantic one.

Among the "fresh young cast" of *Our Winning Season*, a cute blonde named P.J. Soles had caught Dennis's eye. Pamela Jayne had just slid past the age of twenty, but she was the type who could go on playing kooky adolescents long into adulthood.

That belied her sophisticated background, however—born in Frankfurt, Germany, she then went on to live in Casablanca, Venezuela, and Brussels as her father, an insurance executive, opened offices around the world for his company.

P.J. came to New York to attend Briarcliff College, then transferred to Georgetown University in Washington, D.C. to study Russian in preparation for a career in the foreign service. She had acted in high school plays, but had never considered making a career out of it. A summer job running spotlights for the Actor's Studio in New York changed her mind, though. After returning to Georgetown just long enough to pack her clothes, it was goodbye college, hello again New York.

Modeling and advertising work came most readily. P.J. bopped down the streets of New York chomping chicken out of a bucket in an ad for Kentucky Fried Chicken; she flailed the pom-poms as a cheerleader with a dirty uniform in a laundry detergent promo; for Alberto Balsam hair conditioner, she capped a scene in which a hairdresser treated one side of her hair and let the other side remain frizzy with the winsome line, "Can you do the other side now?"

Three years of that kind of work and P.J. was ready for Los Angeles, where the real movie work was to be found. Shortly after moving to the West Coast in 1975, she lucked into a featured role in Brian DePalma's *Carrie*. Remember the girl wearing the red baseball cap at the prom? That was P.J.

The cap was her idea. "I just thought it would be pretty funny," she explained. "I also noticed that all the other girls were trying to look very pretty and I didn't try to compete in that area, so I thought I'd look as much like a tomboy as I could. It was my first movie and I wanted to get noticed. I thought it would work." Her character died in the film, by the way. Not surprisingly, her character also died in her next film, John Carpenter's horror flick, *Halloween*.

A very much alive P.J. Soles began her relationship with Dennis Quaid on the set of *Our Winning Season*, and it led to marriage in 1978 and several minor acting collaborations. P.J. appeared as a prostitute in *The Long Riders*, a film about the Jesse James gang in which Dennis played one of the outlaws, and she had a tiny speaking part in *Breaking Away* as well.

That part came about quite by accident, according to P.J.: "I went away on location with Dennis and they had one entire scene with locals in Bloomington, Indiana, and they cast hundreds of people and they couldn't find anyone to read three lines!" she explained. "Peter Yates asked if I'd do that small part, so I said sure."

Aside from these small backup roles in Quaid vehicles, P.J. also landed several supporting roles in other well-known films. She was Private Wanda Winter to Goldie Hawn's *Private Benjamin*, and she played a tough Army M.P. who became involved with Bill Murray in *Stripes*.

The Quaids led very un-Hollywood lives.

Perhaps they'd hang out at Randy Quaid's house and play music, or go to a basement sushi bar for dinner, or just visit with friends. Weekends, they tried to get away to their spread in Montana and "just watch the cloud shadows roll across the land." There was no partying simply for the sake of hobnobbing with big-shot producers.

Publicly, P.J.'s marriage to Quaid sounded like heaven. She told a reporter in 1981, "We have the perfect relationship. We both understand what the other is going through. The most important thing is that we are not too dependent on our dramatic careers. It is not a matter of life or death whether we get a certain part.

"You cannot make show business your life . . . if we had to leave show business tomorrow it would be okay. Dennis could work on his astronomy or boxing or baseball. I would probably write. We would always have kids . . . I don't think we'd ever get bored."

Certainly not while doing things like taking a two-month round-the-world tour, which Mr. and Mrs. Quaid embarked upon in 1980. Dennis had been feeling a little cheated because, as he said, he had not "gone anywhere for the first twenty-one years of my life."

The trip left him feeling much more complacent about how he lived: "When I got back," he said, "I started realizing how lucky I was, re-

40

ally. Because eight-tenths of the world is walking behind ox carts."

While they were away, P.J.'s agent was contacted about the possibility of her recreating her role in *Private Benjamin* for the impending television series. But P.J. left word that she wasn't interested. Returning home, she also had other distractions: She and Dennis were working with an architect to create their dream home in Montana; they traveled frequently to visit her parents in Arizona; and she spent a lot of time exercising, to stay in shape, as well as cooking, one of her hobbies.

But in comparison to all that, Dennis was moving into showcase roles in movies like *All Night Long* with Barbra Streisand and Gene Hackman, *Caveman* with Ringo Starr, and the highly acclaimed made-for-TV movie *Bill* with Mickey Rooney—and P.J. was stagnating professionally. Unfortunately, what had once been a thriving marriage disintegrated, and by May 1983, Dennis and P.J. were divorced.

Breaking Away, Quaid's next movie after the hopeless *Our Winning Season*, was a breakthrough film for him. Although he had received high marks from the critics for his performances up to that point, none of the projects had been especially illustrious or memorable.

In contrast, *Breaking Away* was nominated for five Oscars, including Best Picture, and it won for Best Original Screenplay. It was also named Best Picture of 1979 by the National Society of Film Critics, and has gone on to become something of a film classic. And all that on the lilliputian production budget of $2.4 million!

Breaking Away is the engaging story of a quartet of working-class kids in Bloomington, Indiana—sons of stonecutters who feel overshadowed on their own turf by the stuck-up preppies attending the university there. Despite the movie's serious themes, it is essentially a warmhearted comedy with some truly inspired scenes and dialogue.

The movie focuses in particular on one of the "cutters," Dave Stoller, and his dreams of becoming a bicycle racer as a way of distinguishing himself. Played by Dennis Christopher, Dave is obsessed with all things Italian because of Italy's predominance in bike racing. In fact, *Breaking Away* was originally entitled *Bambino*.

Dave renames Jake, the family cat, Fellini; listens to Caruso albums; and calls his prototype middle-American mother and father "mama" and "papa." When he reads in a bike magazine that an Italian team is coming to race in Bloomington, he crosses himself and exclaims, "Oh *gracia*, Santa Maria!" His hapless mom then pleads, "Oh, Dave, try not to become Catholic on us."

Dave's Italianization also drives his father crazy. "What's this?" Mr. Stoller asks as he sneers down at his dinner plate one night. "It's sauteed zucchini," says the missus. "It's Eye-tie food!" he explodes. "I don't want no Eye-tie food . . . I know Eye-tie food when I hear it. It's all them 'ini' foods—zucchini, linguini, and fettucini. I want some American food, damn it. I want French fries."

Dennis Quaid plays the substantial part of Dave's buddy Mike, a frustrated former high school football champ seething with resentment against what he sees as his limited opportunities in life. It's summer in the movie, so of course there are ample opportunities for him to take off his shirt. But this role gave Dennis a chance to bare more than his pectoral muscles; he also was able to bare his soul.

One day while he and his cutter buddies are watching football practice on the university campus, Mike eloquently expresses his pent-up bitterness: "Here I am, I got to live in this stinkin' town, and I got to read in the newspapers about some hotshot new star of the college team. Every year it's gonna be a new one. And every year it's never gonna be me. It's just gonna be Mike. Twenty-year-old Mike. Thirty-year-old Mike. Old-mean-old-man Mike. These college kids out here—they're never gonna get old or outta shape 'cause new ones come along every year. They're gonna keep calling us cutters. To them it's just a dirty word. To me, it's just something else I never got a chance to be."

Actually, the role of Mike in *Breaking Away*

is something else that Quaid almost didn't get a chance to be, seeing as he was slated at the time to do another film called Steel, starring Lee Majors. But the financial backers of Steel got a temporary attack of cold feet that lasted just long enough for Quaid to meet with Breaking Away's British-born director, Peter (Bullitt, The Deep) Yates, and accept the part of Mike.

The gem of a screenplay for Breaking Away was written by Yugoslavian-born Steve Tesich, Indiana University class of '65 and one-time winner of its "Little 500" bike race. Director Yates, with whom Quaid was to work again years later in Suspect, explained, "[Tesich] wanted to write a story about kids he identified with, not those he saw on TV or in other films, which are always so condescending to young people. And for my part, I wanted to make a film about class distinction in America. Coming from England, I was always told that it didn't exist here. But of course it does."

It was one of Yates's conditions that there be no stars as the leads in Breaking Away. "I wanted the audience to be concerned only with the story, and not distracted by how well so-and-so looks and acts," he said. That quest took five months of casting, during which "we looked at hundreds of photos, and interviewed scores of people on both coasts."

Critics, who adored the film in general, raved about the casting choices, including that of Quaid as Mike. "The supporting players are uniformly rich in character and nuance, with excellent work by Dennis Quaid, the redneck who dreams of Wyoming and hates the smugness of the college Ivy Leaguers," said Rex Reed.

"Quaid is very good as the ex-quarterback facing a life with no more cheers," crooned *Variety*.

And Janet Maslin of *The New York Times* praised Quaid with the backhanded compliment that "the cutters, who make very convincing misfits, are played by a well-chosen ensemble including Mr. Quaid (Randy Quaid's younger brother, though he bears more resemblance to Jan-Michael Vincent)." That comment irked Quaid enough over the years that as late as 1987, he said to *Rolling Stone*, "What's the biggest misconception about me? That I'm Jan-Michael Vincent."

Breaking Away, which was shot on location in Bloomington with the full cooperation of the university, the city, and hundreds of townsfolk who served as extras, left quite a legacy in its wake. For one thing, the university benefited handsomely from increased alumni donations and prospective student interest.

Secondly, it set a record for the quickest sale of a movie to network television; 20th Century Fox sold *Breaking Away* to NBC for $5 million just three weeks after it won the Academy Award for Best Original Screenplay and only two weeks after it had been sold to theaters for a second run. That meant that instead of the usual three-year lag, *Breaking Away* ran on network television just nine months after its original theatrical premiere, bypassing pay cable altogether.

Lastly, as can be expected from such a popular movie with across-the-board appeal, all three networks were interested in developing it into a TV series. The hour-long pilot, starring Shaun Cassidy as Dave Stoller, premiered on ABC to excellent reviews at the end of 1980. "Attempts were made to get as many of the original cast members as possible," said producer Bert Leonard. "But many of them had conflicting commitments, so we had to move on." Tom Wiggin, a muscular six-footer, filled in for Dennis Quaid in the role of Mike.

Eight episodes were filmed in the college town of Athens, Georgia, but even with Steve Tesich still scriptwriting and Peter Yates producing, the series did not catch on. It was pulled after less than two months on the air, was briefly brought back as a filler during the summer of 1981 baseball strike, then turned belly-up for good.

Almost as if he had a fear of success, Dennis rushed into another clunker after he completed the wonderful *Breaking Away*. The movie was called *Gorp*, a moronic comedy set in a summer camp, with Quaid playing a psycho waiter who stockpiles explosives and a surplus Sherman tank. Once again, *Variety* had a chance to give a scathing review to a Joe (*Our Winning Season*) Ruben project, since he directed *Gorp*, too. "An obvious rip-off of such lucrative youth comedies as *Animal House* and *Meatballs* . . . *Gorp* could be written off as just a poor imitation of a successful type of film were it not so terribly insulting and morally bankrupt," the paper summed up.

And this time, *Variety* didn't even single out Dennis ("Mad Grossman") Quaid for praise. Fortunately, *Gorp* slid quietly into oblivion, leaving the air clean for Quaid's next and far more respectable movie project: *The Long Riders*, his first joint venture with his brother.

▪ 6 ▪

"YOUR FAMILY CAN GET YOU LIKE NOBODY ELSE does," Dennis Quaid once put it quite succinctly. Anyone who has a brother or sister knows that the sibling relationship can be the most difficult—as well as rewarding—of human connections.

For Dennis and his older brother Randy, it has certainly been both. On top of ordinary wrenching family passions, the brothers have had to deal with the complicating fact that they've chosen to make their mark in the same intensely competitive profession.

The Quaids take pains in interviews to emphasize the positive side of their relationship. "Do you and Randy suffer from sibling rivalry?" a reporter once asked Dennis. "Negative," he answered. "We're totally different types. I'm sort of all-American-looking, he isn't—so we don't compete for the same roles. That makes things easier."

Upon close examination, it's noticeable that the brothers do share some basic facial features—prominent cheekbones, assertive noses, almond-shaped eyes. . . . It's just that the proportions were slightly less unusual by the time they got to Dennis.

Randy, almost four years Dennis's senior and, at six-foot-four, also four inches taller, had forged the Quaid trail to Hollywood after spending time studying acting at the University of Houston. He has candidly expressed how much he once resented the prospect of Dennis's muscling in on his turf: "It was kind of rough. I'd sorta made a name for myself and Dennis had stepped in and capitalized on that name. He made more money and did more movies. It bothered me."

Despite their conflict, or perhaps because of it, they were eager to work together. They thought they'd have their shot in *Midnight Express*, with Randy already cast as one of the Americans imprisoned in a rotting Turkish jail and Dennis up for the starring role of Billy Hayes. But the role went to Brad Davis.

Instead, the brothers finally got their chance to team up in the 1980 Western *The Long Riders*—a rendering of the legendary Jesse James story that was most interesting for its use of real-life brothers to portray the fraternal members of the most wanted criminal gang of the 1860s and 1870s.

"The term long rider," the movie's production notes claimed, "is defined as an outlaw who, after robbing a town's bank, rode day and night, using stashed horses as fresh mounts, to escape any pursuers."

The three Carradine brothers—Robert, Keith, and David—played the Younger brothers; James and Stacy Keach were Jesse and Frank James; and Randy and Dennis played Clell and Ed Miller. These daring gang members were folk heroes in the South, but they met a bloody fate when they ventured into hostile territory to pull off a bank robbery in Northfield, Minnesota. They suffered a final betrayal at the hands of another set of criminal brothers, Charlie and Bob Ford, played by Christopher and Nicholas Guest.

Director Walter Hill made the point that *The Long Riders* was actually a "Midwestern," since the James gang was based in Jackson County, in Missouri's Ozark Mountains. The movie was originally supposed to be shot on location there, before the producers discovered that—surprise, surprise—the area had been hit by modernization. So they pushed deeper into the countryside, eventually setting up shop in the mountainous northeastern corner of Georgia.

They also ventured into other parts of Georgia, including the tiny town of Parrott (population

264), a stone's throw from Jimmy Carter's Plains, which they transformed into a reasonable facsimile of Northfield, Minnesota in 1876.

That $200,000 illusion took four weeks to create, during which the production crew filled the town's one street with fifty truckloads of dirt, removed all the utility poles and parking meters, and constructed nineteenth-century wooden facades on all the shopfronts—only to see torrential rains nearly destroy everything they'd built. A tarpaulin actually had to be pulled over the entire street to keep it from turning into a mudbath.

Because of that setback, the Northfield sequences, which were originally scheduled for ten days of shooting, stretched out to four weeks and inflated the original $7.2 million budget to more than $10 million.

Seeing as the James gang also robbed trains in addition to banks, the plan was to film the train sequences in east Texas, along a twenty-seven-mile stretch of railroad that was part of the Texas State Historical Railroad Park. The production company was originally scheduled to spend three weeks filming at this location not too far from Houston—home, of course, to Dennis and Randy Quaid.

But the lush green landscape the director expected had already turned an autumnal brown; the company therefore cut down its stay in Texas to one week.

Still, that week gave Dennis and Randy a

chance to turn the movie into a true family affair. They invited their father, Buddy, to join them on location, and he ended up with a small role in the movie. "Our father was always a frustrated actor," said Dennis at the time. "He used to encourage Randy and me to perform. Now he finally has a chance to perform with us."

But a darker side of familial conflict was portrayed by the Quaids onscreen. In the movie, Dennis's character Ed Miller gets beaten up by Jesse James and booted out of the gang early on because he panicked and turned a routine bank robbery into a shoot-'em-up. (Filming that scene, by the way, yielded Dennis a broken nose. On the tenth take, James Keach accidentally landed a punch that was supposed to just miss him. "We kept doing the scene," remembered Quaid, "but we couldn't use it, because he had such an apologetic look on his face. My nose went to melon, man.")

When Jesse tells Dennis he's out, Dennis poignantly turns to his brother Randy, playing Clell Miller, and begs him to back him up: "You gonna take that offa him?" But Randy turns his back on his brother, saying, "I seen what you done. You may be family and everything, but I ain't sidin' with ya. You're on your own."

Dennis's reaction to Randy during their next scene together—when they run into each other at Jesse James's wedding—reveals how much he had been hurt by his brother's rejection. After introducing his fiancée, Dennis boasts, "I'm doing real fine, Clell. Don't miss you boys none." And in a later scene, when Jim Younger (Keith Carradine) asks Dennis why he isn't joining the gang in their vendetta against the Pinkerton Detective Agency, he replies, "I ain't got no quarrel with the Pinkertons . . . since you boys kicked me out, you can just go ahead and fight your own fights."

In the final analysis, though, Dennis shows that he respects the bonds of kinship and brotherhood. He's in jail on a drunk and disorderly charge when a Pinkerton official offers him several thousand dollars to identify members of the gang when they're caught. "Jesse and his boys are done with you anyway," the Pinkerton man cajoles.

"Well, let me tell you one damn thing," sputters Dennis. "I turn them in and I'm gonna get killed by one of their relatives sure as hell. Now I got six months to go here for bustin' up a place drunk, so I'm just gonna take my chances, awright? Besides, Jesse might just change his mind, and he pays better wages than you do—Pinkerton man!" As much as he resents the gang for turning him out, he knows his allegiance is to them rather than to outsiders.

"Dennis is a genius," David Carradine said about his colleague's performance in The Long Riders. "He reveals things about the character he is portraying with a single gesture." Not to detract from his acting ability, but perhaps Dennis was also able to embody his character so convincingly because of something he had learned from his real-life relationship with Randy—a brother can let you down, but in the end, he's still your brother.

As director Walter Hill, whose previous directing credits included the gang-war chronicle *The Warriors* and *Hard Times*, about prizefighting, put it, "This film, I think, says things about family relationships, that they're special. The use of all the brothers can be perceived as a gimmick but I wanted a family feeling in this movie."

As it turns out, the use of all the brothers in *The Long Riders* was one of the elements the critics, in generally mixed reviews, liked best about the movie. *Variety* called it "an inspired stroke which, given the vicissitudes of Hollywood schedules, billing requirements, and artistic suitability, is a small miracle to have pulled off."

That's an understatement, especially considering that it took the Keach brothers, who cowrote and coproduced the picture, eight years to get it off the ground. Stacy Keach recalled that after each rejection during that marathon search for financing, all the brothers kept agreeing that "our time will come." They hung in there, said Keach, because they were fascinated by the myth of Jesse James's life and death.

Everything came together in, of all places,

Bora Bora, where James Keach was working on the film *Hurricane* when he befriended Tim Zinnemann. Zinnemann, son of *High Noon* director Fred Zinnemann, had never produced a film by himself, but he had enough related film experience and connections that he could finally pull together the pieces that would make *The Long Riders* a reality.

First, he brought Walter Hill on board. And when Hill's movie *The Warriors* turned out to be a hit, United Artists became interested enough to make a deal for *The Long Riders* that included putting up enough holding money to keep the actors available while the script was whipped into shape.

David Ansen of *Newsweek* called the casting of real brothers "Walter Hill's one stroke of novelty. . . . This is more than a publicist's gimmick, however; it gives an extra dimension to the movie's themes of fraternity and family. It is these bonds that Hill mythologizes, not the outlaws themselves, whom he neither glorifies nor condemns."

The rest of the film was viewed less kindly, largely because the director didn't try to say a lot about his characters' inner lives and motivations. "In my films," *New York* magazine reviewer David Denby quoted Walter Hill as saying, "when somebody puts a gun in your face, character is how many times you blink." Commented Denby, "Hill does these moments beautifully. But what a limited idea of character!"

"The film is slow and only vaguely speculative, without much story to give it shape," wrote Janet Maslin in *The New York Times*. While the "bands of famous brothers posture exquisitely," she added, "*The Long Riders* needed something more."

The New Yorker's critic, Roger Angell, however, loved everything about the movie he called "an American beauty. . . . It is a satisfying, beautifully paced and intelligently worked-out retelling of a classic American and movie-Western theme," he said. "The picture is notable for its actors' strong performances, and it should be said at once that a quirk of casting—the employment of four sets of famous or near-famous actor brothers to play four sets of famous outlaw brothers—is effective and absorbing."

Whatever the critics' reactions to *The Long Riders*, the actors had a great time making the film. "It's a situation made to order for sibling, and intersibling rivalry," Hill said during filming, "but so far we haven't had any to speak of."

"There was a lot of love on this picture," elaborated Keith Carradine. "It was easy working together."

Randy Quaid told the *Los Angeles Times*, "I loved working with my brother and all the other guys. It was like one big, happy family."

"It was just like playing cowboys and Indians when you were a kid," said Stacy Keach. "We'd look at each other after every scene and say, 'Isn't this great?' It was all those childhood fantasies—riding horses and shooting guns—come true. I think I could do it forever."

If not forever, Keach hoped he could do it at least once more. A sequel to *The Long Riders* had already been written before the original was even released. Yet how could a sequel be planned to a movie in which nearly all the principals get shot up? With lots of imagination and literary license, that's how.

Though Jesse James got blasted in the back, said Keach, "In the new script, we show Jesse recovering from his wounds and living on to form a Wild West show in which he does an act called 'Crime Does Not Pay.'" Neither, in this sequel, does show business: The script begins in 1910 with Jesse playing his act to a nearly empty St. Louis theater. People have lost all interest in him.

The sequel's life was contingent upon the success of the original. But despite a lavish pre-release publicity campaign for *The Long Riders*, including a $125,000 two-day press junket in Los Angeles, the movie did not spark the revival of interest in Westerns that its producers were counting on. So *Riders II* bit the dust.

At the time *The Long Riders* was made, Randy Quaid's film credits far outstripped his brother's. These side-by-side descriptions appeared in the film's production notes: "RANDY QUAID, who portrays Clell Miller, has been acting so long and so brilliantly it is difficult to realize he's only twenty-seven years old. While a student at the University of Houston, he was chosen for a role in The Last Picture Show and since then has received rave reviews for his work in What's Up, Doc?, Paper Moon, Breakout, Bound for Glory, and The Last Detail, for which he was nominated for an Academy Award.

"DENNIS QUAID, who portrays Ed Miller, is a newcomer to feature films. His powerful performance as Mike in Breaking Away caught the critics' attention as someone to watch. Past film credits include Our Winning Season, I Never Promised You a Rose Garden, and Gorp.

Our Winning Season! Gorp! The stark comparison of his credits with Randy's must have rankled Dennis. After The Long Riders, he threw himself into a frenzy of moviemaking that included a couple of Gorp-like duds, but also some very illustrious projects.

By the time his career path reconverged with Randy's—when they contracted to perform together in the late 1983 production of Sam Shepard's powerful play about raw sibling rivalry, True West—nobody was calling Dennis a newcomer. Especially with his recent performance in the highly acclaimed The Right Stuff, he could now hold his head high.

He might still be Randy's younger brother, but he had also become an accomplished actor in his own right. His burgeoning career was lending increasing weight to a lighthearted quip he had made about the Quaid acting duo a couple of years earlier: "We may not become as famous as the Barrymore family, but if we don't it'll only be because they outnumber us."

He and Randy had even rented back-to-back houses in Los Angeles for a time while Dennis was still married, and their relationship seemed as close as their adjacent properties.

Yet primal sibling hostilities don't merely die or fade away. Sometimes they simply lie dormant, waiting to resurface long after their underlying roots have withered. Then they have to be exorcised violently.

That's what happened with Dennis and Randy early on in the New York run of *True West*, when some problems in a performance one night triggered an actual fight between the two backstage after the show. "We got into a kicking, screaming, shouting, hitting brawl that we'd never been in before," Dennis recalled. "I was in a total rage. I never wanted to be in a play with him again. I never wanted to see him again in my life. I couldn't stand him."

Luckily, fate stepped in just a few minutes later. Dennis needed to use the hairdryer, which happened to be in Randy's dressing room. The brothers were obliged to confront each other again and their talk led to a joyous reconciliation, which Dennis described: "We talked about why we hated each other and why we loved each other and what we envied and admired about each other. We went out and had the greatest time we'd ever had together. That's how it is with sibling relationships."

One of the reasons Dennis had decided to do *True West* was that he wanted the stretch that acting onstage requires. In the theater, he said, "you can take chances, especially off-Broadway, and only two hundred people, instead of two million people, will see you if you happen to fall flat on your face."

"In a movie, all the work is chopped up," he has also said. "You're waiting a lot. I feel like in a movie, the acting is free. It's all the waiting you get paid for; that's the hard part."

Moving to New York City in the summer of 1983, Dennis found a one-bedroom apartment on the Upper West Side, and made his theater debut in a short off-Broadway run of a forgettable play called *The Last of the Knucklemen*.

The New Yorker reviewer gave that play a succinct pan while praising Dennis: "*The Last of the Knucklemen* . . . is about a brawling, sweaty bunch of Australian miners (what they are mining is never revealed) in the bunkhouse of a northwest-Australian mining camp. The hatred of one of them for the boss—the knuckleman (Kevin O'Connor)—is the only thread I could find that holds the rackety action together. The acting, by and large, is good enough . . . near the end, Dennis Quaid, who is better than good enough, treats us to an impressive display of karate, after a lot of general, artless mayhem."

But Dennis didn't have time to dwell on bad reviews. The night after he completed his contracted run in Knucklemen, he opened in True West. For Randy, this was to be his New York stage debut.

The play is about two brothers who start out as diametric opposites, reverse roles midstream, and end up trying to kill each other. Along the way, they prove that they are not so different after all.

There's Austin, described by playwright Sam Shepard as being in his early thirties, neatly dressed in a sports shirt, cardigan sweater, clean blue jeans, and white sneakers. Austin is a successful, established, Ivy League-educated screenwriter.

Shepard describes Austin's older brother Lee, a criminal misfit and social outcast who's been living in the desert, as being in his early forties, wearing a filthy tee shirt, tattered overcoat, dark-blue baggy suit and other Salvation Army castoffs, "pointed black forties' dress shoes scuffed up, holes in the soles, no socks, no hat, long pronounced sideburns, 'Gene Vincent' hairdo, two-days' growth of beard, bad teeth."

You guessed it: Dennis was cast as Austin in the play and Randy played Lee. Austin is housesitting for his mother in a southern California suburb while she's away in Alaska. He's trying to finish up a screenplay when Lee turns up unexpectedly, plainly seething with long-standing resentment against his successful younger brother.

The beer-swigging Lee proceeds to taunt Austin mercilessly. He delivers the ultimate blow when he manages to cozy up to a Hollywood producer and sell him his own screenplay idea instead of Austin's.

Thrilled with his newfound "legitimate" status as a screenwriter like his brother, Lee immediately sits down to flesh out his film script. The only problem is, he can't write. Meanwhile, Austin gets tanked up and goes out to prove that he can be an outlaw just like Lee.

He returns from his burglaries with a cache of stolen toasters and a profound urge to run away from everything. "There's nothin' real down here, Lee! Least of all me!" Austin cries, and begs Lee to take him back out to the desert with him. They strike a deal: Austin will ghostwrite Lee's screenplay and Lee will take Austin out to the desert.

But they barely write one line together before their mother suddenly returns from her trip. Her presence destroys the delicate balance the brothers had worked out. When Lee retracts his promise to take Austin out to the desert, Austin goes berserk and strangles him with a telephone chord. In the final moments of the play, the brothers are locked in mortal combat—different sides of the same character, perhaps, but enemies just the same.

As the Quaids' backstage brawl showed, art and life were closely linked in this play.

In a way, *True West* is probably the best

thing that could have happened to the brothers because it gave them a chance to air all the old grievances. And there were plenty of those, dating back to their earliest days.

Recalling their childhood relationship, Randy said, "There's always a lot of resentment when you're the older one. You've spent four years as the only child, getting all the attention. I still remember the sudden neglect, the feeling of being pushed aside when Dennis came home from the hospital."

"We had spats and fights like all brothers do," Dennis admitted. "In some ways this play reflects our relationship when we were nine and thirteen. We used to fight and tear apart the house and Mom would come home right in the middle of it."

"I used to think about killing him," Randy said. "I used to really beat up on Dennis a lot, unmercifully. I used to love it when he'd scream for Mother and she'd come in and get all upset. I did sort of like to taunt him."

Acting together in True West served as a catharsis in their relationship. "This show has made us closer, because we've gotten all that stuff out," Dennis commented. "Some siblings are too afraid to admit their anger."

But the experience was emotionally exhausting. "Sometimes in New York after the show, I'd just sit back against the wall and say, 'I don't know if I can come back here again tomorrow,' " Dennis confessed. After the play closed in February of 1984, the brothers didn't even see each other for a few months because, as Dennis put it, "There was nothing left to say."

Perhaps there still was unfinished business between them, though, or perhaps they're just masochists. In any case, following a seven-month hiatus, the Quaid brothers reopened in a Los Angeles production of *True West*. This time, they knew full well what they were getting into—how they would have to probe old wounds to bring their characters to life.

But it seems that the Quaids had their major differences ironed out by the time they opened in Los Angeles. Oddly enough, several West Coast theater critics complained that there wasn't enough antagonism between the two onstage. Wrote Dan Sullivan of the *Los Angeles Times*, "Even when Dennis was strangling Randy with the telephone cord, you knew that they really liked each other. Which suggests that it may not be such a good idea to cast two actual brothers in Shepard's fable, at least if they are getting along." When Randy is backing Dennis into a corner, Sullivan continued, his eyes "are as mild as a teddy bear's. And Dennis doesn't make us feel the younger brother's humiliation at how easily he slips back into the victim's role, as if they were still kids."

Los Angeles magazine made a similar assessment. "The current live production at the L.A. Stage Company . . . almost becomes a Sam Shepard play for those who don't like Sam Shepard plays, more *The Odd Couple* than Cain and Abel," wrote the critic, adding that Dennis and Randy "are not only excellent actors but extremely likable chaps. Their natural affinity and Randy's pliable, benign face conspire to lighten up the play."

Dennis and Randy have not acted together since that West Coast production of *True West*. But their relationship obviously survived and emerged stronger from the experience. Dennis has freely admitted that Randy is one of his favorite actors, and there has been talk of finding another joint project. Family is very important to both of them, especially since the death of their father from a heart attack in the spring of 1987.

While Dennis has established himself as a leading man, Randy remains a solid character actor. Paul Muni, a consummate character actor of the thirties, is his role model. "His is the kind of career I'd like to have," Randy has said. "Every role he played was a complete departure from the previous role. I don't know if I could pull off what he did, but I'd like to do something along those lines."

If Vincent Canby of *The New York Times* is any judge, Randy can definitely pull it off. "Like many of the best character actors, Mr. Quaid [Randy] has an appearance that seems to vary from film to film," Canby once wrote. "He is puttylike. His moving, funny performance as the slightly dim-witted sailor, the fellow being escorted to prison in *The Last Detail*, established him firmly in the consciousness of critics.''

For his part, Randy has made peace with the fact that it's not his lot to be cast, as he put it, in "attractive leading-man roles.'' He might as well have said, "in Dennis Quaid-type roles.''

But Randy's list of acting credits can hold their own next to his brother's. He has appeared in such feature films as *The Apprenticeship of Duddy Kravitz*, *Bound for Glory*, *Fool for Love*, and *The Slugger's Wife*.

Lately he's been known more for his television work—especially his one-year stint in 1986 on NBC's *Saturday Night Live*, in which one of his recurring roles was a hilarious impersonation of Ronald Reagan.

Playing Presidents obviously suits him, seeing as another of his major TV roles was his 1987 portrayal of Lyndon Johnson in NBC's three-hour TV movie *LBJ: The Early Years*. He also received an Emmy nomination for his role as Mitch, the hesitant suitor of Blanche Du Bois (played by Ann-Margret) in the television version of *A Streetcar Named Desire*.

• 7 •

DENNIS QUAID HAS THE DUBIOUS DISTINCTION OF
starring in one of the few Barbra Streisand
flops ever. "I don't think the film worked on a
lot of different levels—in the timing of it, in
the relationships," Quaid conceded about *All
Night Long.* "It seemed long to me—it only ran
an hour and a half—but it seemed like two
hours and ten minutes."

Of course, any film also starring Gene Hackman, to say nothing of Dennis Quaid, can't be
all bad. *All Night Long* wasn't terrible; it just
wasn't what audiences expected or wanted to
see from Miss Entertainment herself. Instead of
glitz and fireworks, they got a low-key romantic comedy about ordinary people trying to wring

some meaning from their mundane lives, with Streisand in a basically supporting role.

Hackman plays a stifled drugstore executive who throws a chair through the window during a particularly frustrating meeting with his boss. In a fate worse than getting fired, he gets demoted to night manager of one of the sleazier outlets in the UltraSave chain. To add insult to injury, he learns that his moronic housepainter of a son, played by Quaid, is having an affair with Streisand, an older, married woman and a distant relative to boot.

But when Hackman meets with Streisand to try to put an end to his son's folly, he ends up falling for her himself—leaving Quaid feeling none too charitable toward his father. All ends well when Hackman quits his demeaning job, gets Streisand to move in with him, and starts to put his life back on track.

The critics, searching for the *raison d'être* of this nondescript film and Streisand's out-of-character participation as a homey housewife, generally blamed the incestuous Hollywood scene. *All Night Long*, directed by Belgian-born Jean-Claude Tramont, had been five weeks into production with actress Lisa (*Yanks*) Eichhorn in the housewife role when friction between Tramont and Eichhorn forced a casting change.

Tramont, it turns out, was married to superagent Sue Mengers. And Sue Mengers just happened to be Barbra Streisand's agent. And so it goes. After a few nips and tucks in the script and some reshooting of scenes, Barbra was now the floozy housewife. Tramont, heretofore known mainly as a television and documentary director, protested any insinuations. "My wife and I have been together eleven years," he said at the time. "If she had the ability to force Barbra to do a picture with me, I wish she had used it sooner."

On the other hand, *Variety* pointed out that "Streisand's assumption of the role . . . is unusual in that she actively develops her own projects, has never replaced another actress in a picture, and usually does not appear in a project unless she has the central role." For this departure from her norm, Streisand was reportedly compensated with a cool $4 million plus 15 percent of the gross.

That still only bought one star from New York *Daily News* reviewer Kathleen Carroll, who called *All Night Long* "a dim-witted, bargain-basement movie." Vincent Canby of *The New York Times* marveled that "*All Night Long* is never really boring, if only because one can't believe the high quality of the utter confusion that occupies the screen."

Canby added that Hackman and Streisand together "generate about as much electricity as a movie team as two pieces of wet cardboard being slapped together. . . . Dennis Quaid, as the randy son who introduces pop to pop's new mistress, acts as if he should be in a movie about surfing. Everything in the movie is at sixes and sevens."

Other critics were slightly more generous. David Ansen in *Newsweek* said that although *All Night Long* does not add up to much, "the uneasy but warm rivalry between Hackman and Quaid is played out in fresh and funny encounters."

The New Yorker critic Pauline Kael loved the interaction between Hackman and Quaid: "George [Hackman's character] is particularly funny in his scenes with his muscular, inarticulate son, who grunts like a comic-strip barbarian; to George, this hulk sitting across the table from him is the result of some genetic prank. Hackman and Quaid act with so much rapport that you can feel the father-son bond, whether they're fighting or just glaring at each other."

So Quaid got his share of kudos. But even with heavy promotional muscle behind it—an early screening brought out not only Hackman and the reclusive Streisand, but also such stars as Warren Beatty, Shirley MacLaine, Farrah Fawcett, and Ryan O'Neal—audiences boycotted *All Night Long* as if they were rehearsing for *Heaven's Gate.*

Two months after the film's release in March of 1981, American rentals still had not equalled Streisand's salary, and a *New York Times* West Coast reporter described a Saturday matinee of the film there that drew fewer than 100 viewers to an 800-seat theater, of whom five actually asked for their money back!

All Night Long, wrote Aljean Harmetz, "has joined the select group of movies that audiences actively despise. . . . Advertised as a zany comedy with a poster of Miss Streisand sliding down a fireman's pole, the film is obviously a disappointment to Miss Streisand's fans, and the audience for an askew French-style comedy has never been tempted to sample the movie."

In the sequence of Dennis Quaid's career, 1981 could have been called *All Year Long*. He worked hard and turned in likable, convincing performances. But the movies were either unexpected duds (after all, you wouldn't think Barbra Streisand is paid a fortune to make bombs), or they were innocuous refreshments better suited to bringing home the checks than to making any ten-best lists.

Of course money was, by this time, a serious consideration for Dennis, what with a wife and a house in Montana under construction.

The Montana retreat had actually originated as a lark several years earlier. Driving back to Los Angeles from Bloomington, Indiana (after *Breaking Away*), in a 1954 Chevy he had picked up for $2,000, Quaid passed through paradise—actually Paradise Valley—and knew this was where he had to build his dream house. He drove the rest of the way to L.A. with a deed for twenty-five acres of Montana land in his pocket. "It's a beautiful state," he raved, "and still virgin. If there's anyone who doesn't believe in God, all they have to do is go to Montana."

He'd also come to rely on his Montana getaway for respite from the Hollywood fishbowl, since "most people up there don't bother anybody, and they don't have movie theaters anyway. So the people hardly know who you are."

Quaid's second 1981 release, *Caveman*, marked the directorial debut of Carl Gottleib. Gottleib was a man who knew as much about squeezing money from celluloid as anyone, having cowritten three films that together earned more than $300 million: *Jaws*, *Jaws II*, and *The Jerk*.

Caveman, written by longtime Mel Brooks associate Rudy De Luca, was a prehistoric farce whose immediate crowd-pleasing potential lay in its cast—especially ex-Beatle Ringo Starr and his soon-to-be wife Barbara Bach.

Nobody violently objected to it; in fact, a number of reviewers found it quite amusing. It's just—well, how enthusiastic can you get over a film in which the principals play Neanderthals who grunt and groan their way through the discovery of fire, music, fried eggs, and the thrill of standing upright.

"With all due respect to Ringo Starr," wrote Janet Maslin in *The New York Times*, "the real hero of *Caveman* is not a former Beatle, not the film's top-billed actor, and not even a person at all. The real star is a special-effects dinosaur, one of several such creatures this cheery, playful movie has to offer." The film, she summed up, "is dopey, but it's also lots of fun."

The final product might have been fun, but shooting the film for three months on location around Durango, Mexico wasn't. Costar Jack Gilford said, "The place [where] we made it looked like God created it, took one look, ran away, and never came back. . . . The terrain was rocky. The heat was like stilettos. There was no shade. If you had to go to the john, it was a ten-minute climb down. Then a ten-minute climb back up."

As Ringo's faithful sidekick Lar in the Misfit Tribe's battles with the Hostile Tribe, Dennis gets plenty of beefcake-baring action. If there were Academy Awards for critics, Michael Musto of the now defunct *Soho Weekly News* would surely have won for his description that "Dennis Quaid is shown off like some prehistoric cut of kielbasa, and he fills the role admirably."

Unfortunately for Dennis, he also played straight man for one of filmdom's most nauseating gags, in which Ringo saves him from a huge bug that has settled on his face—by squishing its plentiful guts out right between his eyes.

The cast also included Shelley Long as a cavewoman with a fierce crush on Ringo Starr, and gargantuan John Matuszak, in real life a defensive tackle for the Oakland Raiders, as a fearsome bully. But the dinosaurs still stole the show.

Director Carl Gottleib, for one, was proud of that achievement. "We have the funniest dinosaurs ever filmed," he said. "The audiences love them. United Artists did extensive previews and market research on this picture and the creatures score as high as any of the actors."

Lightweight as it was, *Caveman* made appealing summer fare. "It's a family movie with lots of adventure. It'll be big with kids and mothers. I'm big with kids and mothers," Ringo stated at a press conference. Its box-office earnings were respectable. After four weeks in the theaters and no end in sight, it had already grossed over $10 million.

Quaid's third 1981 film, *The Night the Lights Went Out in Georgia*, is notable as the first time he was able to air his alter ego—Dennis the musician.

Music has always been a consuming passion for Quaid, dating back to his early teens when he started picking out the chords to "Light My Fire" on a $14 K-Mart guitar his grandfather had bought him.

He has said that it even helped him get through the difficulty of being a teenager. "Because I had a lot of time by myself, I'd come home from school, sit and play guitar, make up songs," Quaid said. "It really beats a psychiatrist. Portable therapy, that's what it is."

For a time, he was torn between becoming a musician or an actor. That debate was settled when he auditioned some of his songs for the proprietress of a coffeehouse. "She told me to keep it in my living room," recalled Quaid. "I went back out to my nineteen seventy-one puke-green Duster, and I was crushed. I made a conscious decision right there that, well, I'm gonna be an actor. She probably did me a great favor."

But while acting won out as a profession, music continued to be an important hobby which he has managed on several occasions to integrate into his movie work. As Travis Child, an aspiring country singer in *Georgia*, he plays the guitar and sings his own compositions, "If You Don't Know By Now" and "Amanda Child." (Because *Georgia* was put together on such a tight schedule, he had to write the songs while the film was in production, and the musical numbers were shot at the end.) He also sang country-and-western songs he wrote himself in his film *Tough Enough*, and he crooned his own country-and-Cajun tunes in *The Big Easy*.

The Night the Lights Went Out in Georgia— shot in forty-nine days on a budget of $7.5 million—got its name from the popular ballad composed by Bobby Russell and sung by Vicki Lawrence. The credits say the film is "based on the song," but any resemblance must have gotten lost in the blackout.

The song is about a sister's revenge against a killer who went free after her brother was wrongfully hung for the murder. In the movie version, Travis (Quaid) and his tenacious younger sister/manager Amanda (played by Kristy McNichol) are hopping through stints in rural honky-tonks on their way to conquering the country-music summit of Nashville, Tennessee.

Amanda has big dreams for the talented Travis, but he is as interested in booze and broads as he is in becoming the next Hank Williams. He can never seem to resist the chance to literally charm the pants off any woman he meets, even when he's hightailing it away from the last encounter that most likely landed him in hot water.

Such was the case when he found himself sitting next to a young woman on a bus. He made his play with the quintessential Quaid touch of bad-boy charm that has prompted many to compare him with Jack Nicholson.

"This morning I woke up and I was so bent out of shape I just got down on my knees and said, 'Lord, why do you bring all this misery on me?' " he opened to the woman.

"What did it say?" she asked.

"It said, 'Travis'—that's my name, Travis—it said, 'Hell, I don't know, Travis, something about you just chaps my ass.' "

Nicholson couldn't have done any better. That line, delivered with a glimmer of the irresistible Quaid grin, was all it took to clinch this deal.

Trouble finally catches up with Travis, however, when a sadistic sheriff in one of the backwater towns gets Travis thrown in jail. To make bail, he lands a job bartending at a local roadhouse, and even impresses the locals with an impromptu song session.

But Travis also manages to get the sheriff's blood boiling when he moves in on his girl, resulting in a surprisingly tragic outcome. This led to Buddy Quaid making a cameo appearance at the end of *Georgia* in the rather uncomfortable role of the preacher at his son's funeral.

To find out how Travis might have felt about playing one-night stands in small towns while waiting for his big break in Nashville, Dennis actually tried to put himself in his character's shoes. Before filming began, he went to Nashville to buy a new guitar, then stationed himself and his instrument on the street in front of a club and began to play.

An appreciative crowd formed, and the owner of the club came out. Quaid turned to the man, introduced himself as Travis Child, and asked the owner for an audition. There were no openings in his club, the owner told him, but he gave Dennis some pointers and addresses of people to contact.

On another occasion during filming, Quaid visited a local roadhouse in Chattanooga—the kind of place Travis might play—and again introduced himself as Travis Child and joined in with the band. "People left the dance floor—and left the club," Quaid remembered ruefully.

"But they let me keep coming back. Eventually, I improved. By the time I was doing my own songs, people got up to dance."

Georgia director Ron Maxwell, whose main experience had been in public television, knew Kristy McNichol from directing her in his only other feature film thus far, *Little Darlings*. He had never worked with Quaid before, though, and he was very much impressed by his diligence.

"Dennis Quaid is one of the hardest working, most conscientious actors I've ever worked with," he said. "When you're the real thing, the way he's the real thing, the way Kristy's the real thing, it just comes out on the screen. All you have to do is get it in focus; they bring everything else to it."

Many critics, too, while expressing mixed feelings about the film, had high praise for Quaid. "For young Quaid, lost among all those brothers in *The Long Riders*, this could be a breakthrough," said *The Hollywood Reporter*. "He is handsome, virile, and dynamic (especially when performing with a band), but also displays true warmth and affection in his scenes with McNichol."

"Quaid, the only actor in America who can simultaneously talk, swig Jack Daniels, and put a Marlboro in his mouth, is as big a revelation in *Georgia* as McNichol was in *Little Darlings*," said the *Village Voice*. "Bedroom eyes, postcoital hair, and an insinuating gait define Quaid's

80

1. Dennis said making his $24 million intergalactic epic *Enemy Mine* was "a grueling experience." Certainly looks like it took its toll here.
© PHOTOTEQUE

2. "Who's the best pilot you ever saw?" Dennis Quaid in *The Right Stuff*, of course.
© PHOTOTEQUE

3

3. Dennis and actress
Lea Thompson. It was
Some Kind Of Wonderful
relationship — while it
lasted.

4. "This is New Orleans, darlin', The Big Easy. Folks have a certain way of doin' things down here," Dennis informs costar Ellen Barkin.
© PHOTOTEQUE

4

5

5. "Cavemen" (and woman) Dennis Quaid, Ringo Starr, and Shelley Long.
© PHOTOTEQUE

6

6. Cher's a tough Washington, D.C. public defender, Quaid's a slick dairy-industry lobbyist who ends up on her jury in *Suspect*.
© PHOTOTEQUE

7

7. Quaid graduated from Houston's Bellaire High School in 1972.
© BELLAIRE HIGH SCHOOL

8

8. Dennis gets caught with his pants off but his hat on in *The Night the Lights Went Out in Georgia*.

© PHOTOTEQUE

9. Dennis, with The Grin just itching to bust loose.

10. After five years of marriage, Quaid and actress P.J. Soles called it quits in 1983.

11. One of these days,
Quaid vows, he's going
to take a year off, cut
an album, and go on the
road with his band, the
Eclectics.
© SCOTT WEINER

12. "Breaking Away" —
It's what Dennis did in
1979.
© FOTOS INTERNATIONAL/
PICTORIAL PARADE

11

13. Dennis and Meg Ryan began their relationship when they worked together in *Innerspace*.

© RON GALELLA LTD.

14. Quaid brothers Dennis and Randy saddled up for their first joint project in *The Long Riders*.

© PHOTOTEQUE

▪ 8 ▪

WITH HIS FILM CAREER ROLLING ALONG AT A COM-
fortable pace, Dennis Quaid didn't need to sup-
plement his work schedule with television roles.
Indeed, for an actor with such a long list of
credits to his name, he has remarkably few TV
citations. Three to be exact—if you don't count
the McDonald's commercial he did when he
was just starting out. ("I wasn't very good at
commercials," he confessed. "I didn't have a
commercial personality, I guess. I couldn't say,
'Smells great—that's delicious.' I admire people who can do that even though it's not for
me.")

But his seeming reluctance to resort to television, almost like the old days in which television was considered a lowly third cousin of

feature films, was not due to a lack of offers. In fact, had he succumbed to the lures of television back in the late seventies, Quaid might be best known to millions of people today as the star of *The Dukes of Hazzard*.

That's what CBS was hoping when they offered him ten grand a week to do the show, and the chance to direct to boot. They were dangling some sweet carrots in front of Dennis, but he stood firm in his refusal. "I saw myself in the fifth week of the show, saying, 'What the hell am I doing here!' " he recalled. "And then of course it would be too late to back out. I wasn't willing to compromise with what I felt in my heart."

Two weeks after Quaid turned down the CBS offer, he heard that comedian Freddie Prinze had shot himself. "I suddenly realized if I took the job I would have been Luke the Duke for the rest of my life," he said. "Freddie Prinze saved my life."

As it is, Quaid has participated in only the most sterling of TV specials. The first of these was *Bill*, a 1981 made-for-TV movie based on the true story of a mentally retarded man and his redeeming friendship with a young filmmaker.

Veteran funnyman Mickey Rooney, thanks to a stroke of casting genius, delivered a truly moving performance in his Emmy Award-winning role. He played Bill Sackter, a retarded man who had spent forty-four of his sixty-eight years in a Minnesota state institution.

The audience meets Bill after he has finally been released into the community during the 1960s' rush to liberalize mental-health care. But he's just been eking out a dreary existence as a dishwasher in a country-club kitchen.

Everybody's entitled to a lucky break in life, though, and Bill's comes in the person of filmmaker Barry Morrow, played by Dennis Quaid. He meets Bill during a Christmas party at the country club, where his wife works as a waitress, and he soon realizes the potential goldmine of using Bill as a subject of a documentary film.

But Morrow is not out to exploit Bill; he's sensitive and is concerned enough to become Bill's "buddy" (as Bill calls him) and eventual guardian. He does everything from inviting Bill to dinner at his parents' house to getting him a new pair of dentures.

When the offer of a teaching job at the University of Iowa's School of Social Work forces Morrow to relocate, he arranges for Bill to follow. Bill takes up running a coffee concession in the Social Work building, and his self-reliance becomes so firmly established that when Morrow accepts another teaching job in California, Bill decides to remain in Iowa. "It's my home and I'm on my own now," he declares.

The two-hour Christmastime TV special was capped off by documentary footage of the real

Bill—who was still running his coffee stand at the University of Iowa, and had even made a special honorary visit to the White House when he was named Handicapped Man of the Year in 1979.

Bill is a touching and inspiring piece of work (it won three Emmy Awards), elevated far above the level of mawkish soap opera by the superlative performances of both Mickey Rooney and Dennis Quaid. Rooney is utterly convincing as the feebleminded Bill who has a childlike love and trust of Quaid. And it's one of those ineffable mysteries of fine acting that Quaid as Morrow does not come across as a self-righteous do-gooder, but instead as an ordinary guy who just manages to care a bit more than most mortals.

His totally natural performance inspired the *Christian Science Monitor* critic to gush that the filmmaker Barry Morrow was "played with breathtaking believability by Quaid." The show itself, the reviewer added, was his "absolute favorite of the year."

"Mr. Rooney's performance is beautifully balanced by Dennis Quaid's as Barry Morrow. Mr. Morrow's fascination and occasional exasperation with Bill are never allowed to get sticky," said John J. O'Connor in *The New York Times*, and other reviewers were equally complimentary with virtually unanimous praise.

Quaid thought that *Bill* was an important story that needed to be told, and he was proud of his work. But he also couldn't help remark that "more people saw me in that than any movie I've ever done."

In November of 1983, CBS broadcast a follow-up called *Bill: On His Own*. Once again, Quaid played Barry Morrow, and Bill was played by the somewhat reluctant Mickey Rooney. "I didn't want to do the sequel," said Rooney. "But so many people wanted to know what happened to Bill Sackter's life after he was let out on his own."

In the end, though, he was thankful for his chance to pay tribute to the real Bill Sackter, who died in his apartment in Iowa City at the age of seventy just ten days after the filming of *Bill: On His Own* was completed. And he needn't have worried about the reviewers; often brutal in their attitude toward sequels, they were unexpectedly kind here. *People*'s comment—"The fine acting makes for poignant viewing"—was typical.

This time around, Bill is struggling to adjust to life on his own. He faces a major crisis when his coffee stand burns down, and he takes off to find solace with Morrow in California. But Morrow, it turns out, has been unsuccessful out there. He and his family are teetering on the financial edge, and Bill returns to Iowa. The sequel ends on an up note, however, when Bill, who had recently found out he was Jewish, actually learns enough Hebrew to complete a triumphant Bar Mitzvah ceremony.

Sandwiched in between the two *Bills* was Quaid's only other television performance—in the CBS remake of *Johnny Belinda*. An old chestnut that had had several previous stage and screen incarnations, its best-known version was a 1948 movie starring Jane Wyman in the Oscar-winning role of a deaf farm girl in a Nova Scotian village; Lew Ayres costarred as the country doctor who sees her through a series of traumas.

In this 1982 production, Belinda is played by Rosanna Arquette. Richard (*The Waltons*) Thomas, who'd worked with Dennis in *September 30, 1955*, plays the hero, Bill Richmond—here an idealistic Vista volunteer—who helps her. When he arrives in the community to teach nutrition and farming techniques to the locals, he discovers that Belinda is not retarded, as everyone assumed, but deaf; he sets out to help open up her world.

Dennis Quaid plays the despicable villain of the piece, Kyle Hagar. He's the longtime boyfriend of the district nurse, but she's tired of his brutish ways and turns her affections toward Bill Richmond. In a fit of drunken jealousy after a town dance, Kyle ends up raping the defenseless Belinda.

To play a part so far from his own nature, Dennis tried his best to delve into his character's psyche. "Embedded in all of us is every human act and emotion," he said he discovered. "I spent a lot of time in East Texas where I knew a couple of people like that character in *Johnny Belinda*. I asked myself, 'What kind of pain is he going through?' You've got to relate to what trouble he has. Villains aren't villains to themselves."

It would seem to be a totally thankless role that Quaid took on in *Johnny Belinda*. But, characteristic of his talent, he managed to bring a power and believability to the part that distinguished him and elicited kudos from the critics. "Miss Clark [the actress who played the nurse] and Mr. Quaid have the grittier parts and very nearly steal the show," wrote John J. O'Connor in *The New York Times*.

As for other TV work, Dennis Quaid is not likely to stay in one place long enough to take on a role in a regular television series. As an actor constantly looking for new horizons and new challenges, he shuns the stagnation that can result from playing the same role week in, week out. "I want to play as many different roles as possible," he has declared.

"Movies are great, like having a job for three months, then going on to the next thing," he has also said. "I get to go to this place, to be this person, to live this life. My favorite part is the research.

"When I go to a location, go into a town, I'm there for three months and pretty much get carte blanche wherever I go. Like when I did *The Right Stuff*, I got to go to NASA, and go through everything. Any door that said 'Authorized Personnel Only,' I would just open up. It's a great excuse for finding out about the world instead of going to the library."

Dennis is a dilettante—in the best sense of the word. As he moves from role to role gaining new experiences, he might even earn the title of Renaissance man.

• 9 •

THE YEAR 1983—ALMOST "THE YEAR OF QUAID"—
began for Dennis with the release of *Tough
Enough*. To prepare for his role as a down-on-
his-luck singer/songwriter who enters amateur
boxing matches in hopes of winning prize
money, Quaid simply did more of what he had
being doing all along; at eighteen, he had taken
up boxing as an alternative to dancing to keep
his actor's muscles toned.

Boxing had become such a passion that he
even had a fleeting dream of competing in the
Olympics, until he realized that he lacked the
"killer instinct" to go all the way. Nevertheless, he continued to enjoy it as a hobby and as a
surefire way to shed Hollywood pretensions
and get down and regular with the guys in the

gym. "They don't treat me differently there," he said in 1983. "To them, I'm still the skinny white boy. Nothing is going to change that."

But something else did change. Several years ago, Dennis gave up boxing altogether after getting a look at Muhammad Ali in a Santa Monica gym. "He was . . . sad, man. He was slow," Quaid said. "Now I'm into yoga and golf."

Back on the set of Tough Enough just outside Dallas, Quaid found himself slugging it out for up to twelve hours in 100-degree-plus summer heat, losing several pounds a day in the bargain, but gaining the supreme admiration of his costar, the late veteran actor Warren Oates.

"You see that?" the incredulous Oates asked Houston Post film critic Joe Leydon when he visited the Tough Enough set. Oates was referring to Quaid's strenuous boxing warm-up before the shooting session began. "He works like this every day for hours and hours before every shot. He's gettin' ready, loosenin' up—and right now, he's just goin' over there to sit in the corner.

"I know Dennis's total heart is in this. This kid is absolutely tremendous. I think he and Timothy Hutton are gonna be the important young men comin' up in the next ten years."

Dennis laconically summed up the strain of making Tough Enough by saying, "It was pretty damn taxing." But the physically demanding part left no scars; that is, if you don't count the off-the-set fracture he suffered in his hand when he whacked a spiderweb hanging over the entrance to his Texas hotel room!

Tough Enough was a perfect Quaid vehicle: It gave him a chance to display those by-now famous rippling abdominal muscles and his musical talents (his character in the film keeps boxing because the fight promoter promised him a chance to sing on national TV, which he eventually gets).

Unfortunately, it wasn't a very good movie. Harry Haun in the New York *Daily News* gave it a humiliating half a star ("*Tough Enough?* Believe me: You aren't tough enough to endure the torture and tedium accompanying this tired, reeling, punch-drunk yarn.")

Janet Maslin of *The New York Times* called it "a very dull boxing movie with no other distinguishing features." About the nicest comment she could muster was that "Mr. Quaid and a number of the other actors here . . . have been better in other movies."

"It would have been rather pleasing to have something happen to that appealing Quaid that could be taken seriously," mused Archer Winston in the *New York Post*. "After all, he does pick a good guitar, sing well, and look muscularly impressive. His personality has 'legs,' so why don't they let him go instead of crawl into this plot corner and die."

People magazine didn't like the movie much better than other reviewers, but it did take pains to emphasize Quaid's talent: "His energy and humor give his scenes spontaneity, and his exchanges with his young son [Christopher Norris] are delightful. . . . If he can work such magic with a derivative script like this, imagine what he ought to be able to do with *The Right Stuff*, the upcoming film of Tom Wolfe's astronaut saga, in which Quaid is cast as Gordon Cooper."

People was correct to look forward to Quaid's brilliant performance in *The Right Stuff*. But first, Quaid showed up in an unfortunate project that preceded it in the theaters: *Jaws 3-D*.

Everyone makes career mistakes when they're starting out; an actor wants exposure, needs to work, needs to eat, and so accepts roles in movies like *Gorp*. But for those who start getting lucky breaks, as did Quaid, there usually comes a time when they must decide there are some things they won't do just for money or sheer commercial appeal anymore.

Sometime after its release, even Quaid acknowledged that *Jaws 3-D* may have qualified as one such project. "*Jaws 3-D* wasn't all that well-written and it didn't scare me. It looked like the shark was on downers," he told *The Aquarian*.

A year later he said, "I don't like talking about it because I don't think *Jaws 3-D* worked as a movie. I'm not crazy about it. The story wasn't there. The way to interest an audience in that type of story is to show what the shark did to the people, how this experience affected them. *Jaws 3-D* just didn't have that substance—and it was very predictable."

But Quaid is no Benedict Arnold; he did not betray the film before it came out. Quite the contrary, he dutifully promoted it, telling reporters at the time, "The script is really exciting. My role is a bit like Richard Dreyfuss's in the first film."

And: "It's a commercial film with a good script and characters. The 3-D effects are state-of-the-art and, of course, the shark is bigger [than in the previous *Jaws* films]." That amazing twelve-foot-long shark head also could breathe air through its gills, roll its eyes back, and curl its lips into a snarl.

Jaws 3-D—budgeted at $16 million, the highest yet for a 3-D picture—was meant to stand (or fall) on its own; the story was not made as a sequel to pick up where its predecessors left off. Said producer Rupert Hitzig, "The only resemblance to the other two films is that *Jaws 3-D* incorporates the same tested villain, the shark." The special effects were meant to "add a new dimension to photographic reality."

They also added a new dimension to the problems that this producer had to contend with. For one thing, a new twin-lens camera system developed especially for the project was two weeks late in delivery, and filming had to start without it.

Secondly, since neither Hitzig, the director (Joe Alves), nor the cinematographer (James

Contner) had worked with 3-D before (and Alves, the acclaimed production designer on the first two *Jaws* films as well as *Close Encounters of the Third Kind*, had never directed a feature film before), they relied on three 3-D experts they hired for advice. And the problem was that these experts continually disagreed on the right approach.

Even something as elementary as which film stock to use caused problems; according to the *New York Post*, cast and crew had to spend extra days reshooting scenes that had not been shot with the correct 3-D film!

Another difficulty was caused by the fact that about a third of *Jaws 3-D* takes place underwater. Most of it was shot in the Orlando marine life park, Sea World of Florida. The actors had to learn to scuba dive, and they got the waterlog blues from spending so much time submersed during filming.

"You're just sitting underwater, breathing air and watching your bubbles float up," Quaid said. "We were sometimes in the water for as long as eight hours—and it was winter so the Florida water was cold! But sometimes dolphins would come visit and let us hang on for rides. *That* was fun!"

While Dennis's motives for participating in *Jaws 3-D* might have been questionable, director Alves's reasons for hiring him were solid. "We cast the actors not only for their talent," he said, "but also for their lack of temperament. We knew it would be a long, hard shoot, the water would be cold." And Dennis had a well-deserved reputation of being easy to work with.

He plays the part of underwater construction engineer Mike Brody, who's supposed to be the grown-up son of the heroic *Jaws* and *Jaws II* shark-killer, Roy Scheider. He's also the boyfriend of a marine biologist, played by Bess Armstrong.

They're both employed by Louis (*An Officer and a Gentleman*) Gossett, Jr. as the owner of an underwater park who's a bit distressed to discover that a great white man-eating shark has slipped into his park's lagoon behind some waterskiers.

Lou Gossett's most memorable line was probably, "Move dat fish"—which gives you some idea of the quality of the script. Like the rest of the cast, Quaid was not given much to work with.

But always the trooper, he approached that limitation as a challenge. During filming, he told a Florida reporter, "The character's hard because he's such a straight guy. I had to find an inner life for him. I went around with men from the engineering department at Sea World on their rounds. I also got some knowledge from engineering books. He has a relationship with a girl. I'm trying to make it [the role] very personal."

Universal, the distributor of *Jaws 3-D*, had

begun hyping the film months before filming had even started, papering theater lobbies with posters of a voracious shark and proclaiming, "The third dimension is terror." But by July of 1983, right before the film's release, *People* magazine was saying that "word of mouth on the film is lukewarm."

They even quoted producer Rupert Hitzig expressing his doubts: "We could use another year on the film. If we did it over again it could be fantastic. Right now, it's only very good." It's not often you hear a producer criticizing his baby before it's even born!

Less than a month before *Jaws 3-D* opened, director Joe Alves also started making public excuses. He admitted to Gene Siskel in the New York *Daily News* that he was worried: "The ads are saying that we're going to put the shark right into the audience's lap. Now, I know if we do that, we'll really have a great picture and make millions, but we don't have it yet. We're trying, but it's almost impossible to do."

Then Alves had his film editor, Randy Roberts, explain the reason to Siskel. It was something about a shark being too big for optimum 3-D special effects. "What works best in 3-D," Roberts said, "is a narrow cylindrical object, like a pencil or pool cue."

Now you tell us! After building a life-sized mechanical shark and a 1.5 million-gallon, solar-heated tank with a special filtration system to keep the water clear to film him in!

Universal, too, seemed to be getting queasy about *Jaws 3-D*'s prospects; they decided not to have any advance screenings before the film's opening day. But they did finally premiere it with a bang at Sea World of Florida. The gala fifty-dollar-a-head benefit for Find the Children and the Adam Walsh Foundation for missing children was held in the 850-seat Undersea Fantasy Theater, converted for the night to 3-D. Dennis Quaid attended, along with other members of the cast and production staff.

Predictably, despite all the producer's protestations that *Jaws 3-D* was not a cheap, gimmicky, exploitation film, reviewers acted like that's exactly what it was. They almost unanimously hated it. "Does anybody give a flying shark fin about the 'plot' of *Jaws 3-D*?" asked *Newsweek*'s critic David Ansen rhetorically. "We all know what we're in for: a bit of the old bite and run."

And: "Yes, folks, just when you thought you were safe from being scared to pieces by a man-loving shark, they've dreamed up *Jaws 3-D*, a movie that allows you to closely inspect the dental work of a shark," sniffed Kathleen Carroll in the New York *Daily News*.

"The film has no fins and should drown quickly," predicted *Variety*.

Quaid had jumped into the *Jaws 3-D* deep end, hoping simply for one big commercial hit to catapult him over the top. Instead, he learned a valuable lesson that would affect his whole career.

"I asked myself, 'Why am I an actor?' " he admitted. "Because I like creating a character. That was just crap what I was doing. So I sold the house and went to New York to start over. I lost all my money. . . . It was the most discouraging point of my life."

Dennis not only sold his house in Los Angeles, he also dumped the half-finished dream house he had been building in Montana. "It kind of symbolized my life at the time," he said. "I was broke. When you're young your head gets away from you."

Quaid might have also mentioned that he was getting divorced from his wife, P. J. Soles, at around this time. On the brighter side, however, he resurfaced from *Jaws 3-D* with a new girlfriend, a young waterskiing member of the cast named Lea Thompson.

Jaws 3-D, which began filming in the fall of 1982, was Thompson's first feature film. She was a cute twenty-one-year-old with a steely determination honed by years of rigorous dance training. Originally from Minneapolis, Minnesota, Thompson was the youngest of five children born to an insurance-agent father and a mother who took up nightclub singing after her divorce from Lea's father when her daughter was eight.

Lea began studying dancing soon after, encouraged by her artistic mother and inspired by an older brother who was with the Minnesota Dance Theater. "Dance was the love of my life," she said. "I was so dedicated that my peers thought it was unnatural."

After she graduated from high school, she won a two-year scholarship to the Pennsylvania Ballet in Philadelphia, then another to the Ballet Repertory, the American Ballet Theater's second company in New York.

But the dreadful reality of her physical limitations was beginning to dawn on her. At five-foot-four, she realized "that I would never be the best. My legs were not long enough to make it as a Balanchine dancer and I did not want to settle for less than the top." After eleven years of ballet training, Thompson found an agent who landed her a series of Burger King TV commercials, and then a small part in *Jaws 3-D*.

The fairy tale experience of meeting the man to whom she later became engaged on the set of her first film, was, in her words, "Pretty Hollywood, isn't it?"

"Dennis is the greatest person, kind and hardworking," she also said.

"I'm very much in love. He's very special," she gushed to another reporter.

Dennis was likewise smitten. "She's devoted to her work, and has a great sense of humor," he said. "But I guess the thing that most attracted me was her soul. She has a great soul."

In May of 1984, they announced their engagement. But Dennis was deeply involved in his career, and Lea had no intention of letting hers languish either. After they met, she launched into a heady succession of prime roles in the movies *All the Right Moves*, *Red Dawn*, *The Wild Life*, *Back to the Future*, *Yellow Pages*, and *Space Camp*.

What time they had together was spent visiting each other on their respective movie sets or grabbing a few precious days when both of them miraculously happened to be in between projects at the same time.

Time was at such a premium that they even had to negotiate who would accompany whom on the promotional rounds if they both had films opening concurrently, as was the case with his *Dreamscape* and her *Red Dawn* in August of 1984.

About the only one making hay from this situation was the phone company. "You should see his phone bills," Thompson said. "It's tough with him working and me working. We don't get to see one another as often as we'd like. . . ."

Especially if the schedule Thompson described in July 1985 was any indication: "We were on separate continents for eight months. I was in Europe making *Yellow Pages* while he did a play here. Then I came back here to make *Back to the Future* and he went to Germany to do *Enemy Mine*. We got together once when we both flew to New York."

Finally, reality reared its head again. By July of 1987, the couple had split up, reportedly due to the problems of too much time spent apart in pursuit of their individual careers.

"We're still great friends. But it's tough," Dennis said. Tough, but not tragic; it wasn't that long before Quaid found love again—with yet another costar in one of his movies.

• 10 •

"IT WAS THE GREATEST LOVE AFFAIR OF MY LIFE,"
Dennis Quaid said in the fall of 1983. No, he
wasn't referring to his budding romance with
Lea Thompson; he was talking about his in-
volvement with the epic film, *The Right Stuff*.
"When my hair grew out," he said, "I cried."

Not a very manly thing for an actor portraying a tough test-pilot-turned-astronaut to do.
Then again, Quaid was probably just speaking
with the characteristic hype inherent in his
role as hotdog flying ace Gordon Cooper, the
youngest of the seven Mercury astronauts and
last to be launched into space. It was Quaid as
Cooper who nearly stole the show in *The Right
Stuff* whenever he turned to someone and de-

manded, "Who's the best pilot you ever saw? Damn right, you're looking at him."

What a role, what a movie, what a chance for Dennis. Nobody realized that better than Quaid himself. He had read Tom Wolfe's dazzling chronicle of the origins of America's space program along with the other 1.2 million readers who had made the 1979 book a phenomenal bestseller.

He had picked up a copy while in Dallas filming *Tough Enough*, his interest whetted by the fact that every day on the way to location, fighter jets from the local Air Force base would zoom overhead. "The Blue Angels [the crack precision performing team] would come like fifty feet off the ground at four hundred miles an hour," he said. "Wow! 'Jeez, that would make a great movie,' I thought."

Quaid devoured Wolfe's opus in two days, and by the time he put it down, he knew that if they ever made a movie of *The Right Stuff*, he just had to play the part of astronaut Gordon Cooper. Said Quaid, "He was the only guy I knew I had a chance for; he was the youngest and he also fell asleep on the launching pad just before blast-off, which I thought was pretty cool."

Aside from the acting possibilities, *The Right Stuff* was appealing on other levels. For Quaid, the would-be astronaut who grew up in the shadows of the Johnson Space Center ("I'd wanted to be an astronaut since I was a kid," he claimed), it was a chance to relive his boy-hood fantasies. He had never forgotten the awe he felt sitting in his kindergarten classroom watching Alan Shepard's historic space flight from takeoff through splashdown. And for Quaid the astronomy buff, it brought those starry heavens he loved to contemplate from his back-yard (with his fourteen-inch reflector telescope and other photographic equipment) that much closer.

So when Quaid, twenty-seven at the time, learned that *The Right Stuff* was being made into a movie, the ordinarily laid-back, come-what-may actor sprang into action. Here was a project really worth fighting for. He immedi-ately flew out to San Francisco for an audition—only to get the "thank you very much for coming but you're too young for the part" brush-off.

But he got a reprieve when *The Right Stuff* director Philip Kaufman, who had decided he wanted one relative youngster in his astronaut lineup after all, saw *The Night the Lights Went Out in Georgia* and was impressed with Quaid. The dream part of a lifetime soon became his. And Quaid knew he was damn lucky to get it, since the next youngest guy in the cast was thirty-five. "It was one of those rare times you want something so bad and you actually get it," he said.

The Right Stuff was, to put it mildly, a daunt-ing project for everyone. First of all, there was the difficulty of translating Tom Wolfe's brilliant but idiosyncratic and choppy tale into screen language. Wolfe's book is grandly ambitious in its scope (it covers not only the behind-the-scenes story of America's first astronauts, but also of their predecessors, the legendary test pilots), its characterizations (Wolfe turns a jaundiced eye toward everyone from Lyndon Johnson to "our" German scientists who developed the first space capsules), and its themes.

Dominating that category are Wolfe's questions about the nature of celebrity in this country and, especially, about the nature of "the right stuff." As far as celebrity goes, Wolfe didn't seem to have much trouble identifying the bad guys—it was the press, those ubiquitous journalists who mercilessly bully and distort. "The press is very important in this story, because the press is the singer of the song, the maker of the myth of the heroes," Philip Kaufman has said. "Often they don't sing the song the right way, or they sing the wrong song."

As for the "right stuff," even Wolfe, with his fabulous command of expression, had a hard time putting his cursor on that one. It was a quality that the best among the "brotherhood" of the great fighter-jocks possessed—and knew they possessed—but never really talked about.

Wolfe tried to describe it. He said it was "the uncritical willingness to face danger." It "involved bravery. But it was not bravery in the simple sense of being willing to risk your life. The idea seemed to be that any fool could do that, if that was all that was required, just as any fool could throw away his life in the process.

"No, the idea here (in the all-enclosing fraternity) seemed to be that a man should have the ability to go up in a hurtling piece of machinery and put his hide on the line and then have the moxie, the reflexes, the experience, the coolness, to pull it back in the last yawning moment—and then go up again *the next day*, and the next day, and the next day, even if the series should prove infinite—and, ultimately, in its best expression, do so in a cause that means something to thousands, to a people, a nation, to humanity, to God."

Clearly, adapting such a far-reaching book for the screen was no small task. So producers Robert Chartoff and Irwin Winkler—independents who were riding high after their successes with *Rocky* and *Raging Bull*—did the reasonable thing and came up with a reported $750,000 to hire a screenwriter with no small reputation. William Goldman was a highly acclaimed veteran, noted for his screen adaptations of *All the President's Men* and *A Bridge Too Far* as well as the adaptation of his own novel, *Marathon Man*, and the screenplays for *Harper* and *Butch Cassidy and the Sundance Kid*.

Goldman took the poetic license of cutting out a good chunk of the Wolfe tale. He focused on the story of the astronauts and left out the part that dealt with that test pilot extraordinaire, Chuck Yeager, the first man to break the sound barrier. United Artists, the film's distributor, okayed the project, but Winkler and Chartoff had their reservations. And when they contacted Philip Kaufman as a possible director, he echoed those doubts.

Phil Kaufman was not a man with as weighty a track record as Goldman's. His best-known directing credits were for *The Wanderers*, a Bronx-set gang movie, and the well-received remake of *Invasion of the Body Snatchers*; he had also had a hand in writing the scripts for *The Outlaw Josey Wales* and *Raiders of the Lost Ark*.

Nonetheless, Kaufman was hired—bolstered by a thirty-five-page memo in which he laid out his vision that *The Right Stuff* be "a search film, a quest for a certain quality that may have seen its best days"—and Goldman quit. Since Tom Wolfe had no intention of penning a screenplay to replace Goldman's, that left any number of other potential screenwriters, as well as Kaufman. Kaufman decided to do it himself.

He had a first draft ready in just eight weeks, and things were moving along nicely. Casting began with the tapping of playwright/actor/heartthrob Sam Shepard to play Chuck Yeager. Yeager himself was signed on as a consultant. Locations were scouted. The revised script was sent on to United Artists.

It just so happened, however, that the script arrived on United Artists' doorstep right about

110

the time they released the $36.5 million *Heaven's Gate*. Michael Cimino's film, for those who like to snicker at Hollywood's folly, will be remembered as one of the biggest, most expensive, most embarrassing flops Tinseltown had ever conjured up.

United Artists was understandably gun-shy for the moment. "United Artists backed out," said Kaufman. "They were afraid if a Western like *Heaven's Gate* cost so much and fell so hard, *The Right Stuff* would be doubly deadly."

Enter the Ladd Company, a mini-studio within Warner Brothers, helmed by forty-six-year-old golden boy, Alan Ladd. At least, he had been a golden boy during his three years as president of 20th Century Fox, where they remembered him fondly for a little project called *Star Wars*. He was doing considerably less well with his own company, which was to release such commercial disappointments as *Outland*, starring Sean Connery, and the only modestly profitable *Body Heat*.

The Ladd Company agreed to Kaufman's demands: "I direct. No superstars, seventeen-million-dollar budget, primary shooting in San Francisco." By October of 1981, *The Right Stuff* was back on the right track.

The next item on the agenda was casting the principal roles of the seven Mercury astronauts. "The guys had to work so closely together, pal around, look right, that I had scouts look at about a thousand actors," Kaufman told the *New York Post*.

"I was looking for an almost obsolete type of fifties' guy who was not affected by a modern look," he also said. "I wanted guys who were very rugged, very tough, very honest, open guys with a clean-cut quality."

All of Kaufman's casting choices were right on the money—including those of Ed Harris as John Glenn, Scott Glenn as Alan Shepard, and Fred Ward as Gus Grissom. But none were more so than Dennis Quaid as brash, cocky, good-natured, unflappable, "hotdog" flyman Gordon Cooper, Gordo to his friends.

Of course, there was a bit of the hotdog in Dennis already. And Quaid immediately set out to internalize the aspects of Cooper that were different from himself. Toward that end, Dennis arranged a meeting with Cooper through Jim Rathmann, a Chevrolet dealer in Cape Canaveral who was mentioned in Wolfe's book.

Rathmann had become chummy with the Mercury astronauts while they were based at the Cape, giving them Corvettes and turning them on to auto racing. So when Quaid went down to the Cape to visit NASA (National Aeronautics and Space Administration) and research where the whole space program began, he made sure to look up Rathmann to get some inside stories on the astronauts. Rathmann called Cooper and set up a meeting.

Cooper, then fifty-six, had quit NASA in 1970

when his bosses ordered him to withdraw from a stock-car race in Daytona. He was now living in Encino, California, and a partner in a West Coast firm that was working on developing a low-cost alcohol fuel for jets and racecars. As the movie *The Right Stuff* presaged, his first marriage had ended in a bitter divorce after the couple could no longer keep up the happy front that America expected from its astronauts. He was now in the eleventh year of his second marriage to a woman eighteen years his junior, with whom he had been able to have two children after reversing a 1959 vasectomy. ("In the days when no one knew what we would encounter in space," Cooper told *People* magazine, "we were warned that our children might be mutants because of the effects of radiation.")

Quaid met with Cooper before Kaufman issued the edict that none of the actors were to meet with the real men they were portraying. "Phil didn't want us to limit ourselves by seeing these guys as they are today, since that could be different from what they were then," explained Lance Henriksen, who played astronaut Wally Schirra. But Quaid, always the eager beaver, had already jumped the gun.

Step one in Dennis's transformation into Gordo was to have his light tresses curled, dyed red, and clipped off. The result looked like realistic military issue—"It sort of had all those holes in it . . . like my head had been bounced around inside a cockpit," Quaid said. Then he changed the way he walked into what he called "a swing-march kind of stride," learned an Okie drawl, and began to hold his mouth differently.

After he had the physical characteristics more or less down, Quaid started in on acquiring some of the knowledge and skills that Cooper had. He couldn't very well become an astronaut, but he did do the next best thing—learn to fly. "I figured I might as well," he said. "All those guys used to be test pilots and have certain attitudes about things. For some reason, they cross their arms the same way. They're very exact in the way that they talk. They have to be in control of themselves to do what they do, to go out and put their life on the line."

Perhaps more to the point, Quaid told *Flying* magazine, "Every pilot in America will watch this movie and I just had to get it right." At the same time, he had to overcome his mother's nervousness about his flying a plane, not to mention his own fear, which stemmed from the fact that his brother-in-law had been killed in an airplane crash. He even had a nightmare about crashing into a huge cliff that was inauspiciously situated directly at the end of a runway.

But Quaid proved that, like the character he was playing, he had a good dose of the right stuff. At the Van Nuys Airport in California, he was put under the tutelage of seventy-seven-year-old Bud Whalen, who took Quaid up in his old Piper Cherokee 140 and taught him to fly the old-fashioned way: by instinct rather than by instruments. They went up three or four times a week, and Whalen couldn't help being impressed. "Dennis was very ambitious," he reported. "He reminded me of the stunt men who want to learn how to fly and say, 'Just show me how to do it.' He's a great guy, very down-to-earth. I'd like to have him for a son."

Quaid conquered his fears so well that he earned his single-engine pilot's license and tried to enlist in the Air Force Reserve, only to discover he was six months too old and needed the college degree he had never obtained.

But civilian flying has remained a passion of his—so long as the weather's clear. On one of his first trips with passengers, he flew from Los Angeles to Las Vegas and got caught in down drafts near a thunderstorm, losing 2,500 feet of altitude. That experience taught him a basic lesson in aviation: "I just won't fly in bad weather. Period. It's no fun. You get tossed around, and flying ought to be fun."

While Quaid was visiting NASA and Cape Canaveral and learning to fly for his role in The Right Stuff, Kaufman was trying to cope with some of the enormous logistical problems the film posed.

There were a mammoth 135 speaking parts to cast and film, plus 200 nonspeaking parts and 5,000 extras. Dozens of cars spanning two decades were needed, including seven 1962

Lincoln Continental convertibles. Some of the vintage aircraft called for were no longer available, and the ones that were needed frequent repairs.

Because Kaufman wanted to blend actual historical scenes into his new version of reality, there were literally miles of stock footage from NASA and the National Archives that had to be reviewed, culled out, and matched to the new film. (Some of that archival footage, transferred onto videotape and catalogued into a computer for easy recall, also served as an additional research tool for the actors trying to recreate the original righteous brothers and their milieu.) And the tricky soundtrack called for such complex and expensive special effects as sonic booms.

All that took about two years from script to screen, of which a long eight months was spent in actual filming. Those months provided ample opportunity for the actors to *become* their characters as much as possible.

"Everyone really took on the role that their astronaut counterparts had in the real program," said Lance Henriksen, describing how the actors began to break up along military lines just as the originals had. "Scott and I were the academy men, the Annapolis graduates," he explained. "We tolerated Ed Harris [playing John Glenn] as this crazy marine. We allowed Charles Frank [as Scott Carpenter] to think he was a 'real' Navy officer. But we looked at the

Air Force pilots [Fred Ward as Gus Grissom, Dennis Quaid as Gordon Cooper, Scott Paulin as Deke Slayton] as basically flakes."

Off the set, the actors would hang out together in a bar called Tosca's, which Quaid has remembered fondly: "We would go down there at night and play pool, drink, and talk planes. We all had buzz haircuts ... I lived, ate, and breathed *The Right Stuff* for eight months." Run by a salty woman named Jeannette, Tosca's was as close as you could get in San Francisco to the Edwards Air Force Base hangout, Pancho's Fly Inn (alternately known as the Happy Bottom Riding Club), that had been an institution among thirsty test pilots.

Some of the actors identified so strongly with their characters, said Henriksen, that they even felt an initial resentment toward Chuck Yeager. Wolfe's book described how Yeager and other test pilots had looked down on the astronauts as lab rats, not much better than the chimp who was first sent into space.

When the actors first met for a briefing with Yeager, Henriksen recalled: "He started in with the old business about 'Spam in a can' and 'a monkey made the first flight.' By the time he was through, I was standing in the room's farthest corner with my back to him and my body in a totally closed position.

"Scott Glenn didn't even show up. The next day, I asked him why, and he said, 'Who wants to hear about obsolete airplanes?' That was ex-

117

actly the attitude Alan Shepard had toward guys like Yeager who put down the astronauts."

Quaid, however, was enthusiastic about meeting Yeager right from the start. "In the movie," he said, "Gordon is a protégé of Yeager and sort of idolizes him. I just watched Chuck Yeager and copied what he did—he does a thing with quarters, rolls them over his fingers all the time. Fighter pilots have many movements in common, like they all wear big wristwatches."

With *The Right Stuff* scheduled for nationwide release on October 21, 1983, everyone was working right down to the wire to meet that deadline. A huge amount of interest in the film had already been generated by a massive pre-release publicity campaign, including lots of statements from Kaufman.

"We've tried to show just what the astronauts went through; the panicky, confused, and exciting way America entered the Space Age. Fingers crossed, eyes blinking, the works," he said in a *New York Post* article. "But we're not debunking these men. This movie demonstrates how they rose above not only their personal problems but the public hype to become *real* heroes."

"We wanted to delve into the past to find the roots of the future," he also said. "Everyone else is out doing *Star Wars*/interplanetary things in the far-flung future. I thought it was time that people became interested in the first vessels and the explorers who broke these barriers.

"The actors were great . . . they really *became* those seven guys. I remember watching Ed Harris playing pool with Lance Henriksen and hearing them call each other 'Wally' and 'John.' It went that far."

Recreating reality in meticulous detail, added Kaufman, "became an adventure for us all. The actors loved it. They're all pretty physical guys . . . they all got into doing their own stunts with all the training equipment. They were so excited that, after awhile, it was like Christmas. We had to pull them away from their toys before they wasted the whole day."

That certainly applied to Dennis, who was actually looking forward to his ride in the "vomit comet," a jet carrier used to simulate the feeling of weightlessness. He got to keep his lunch when they decided to use documentary footage of the real astronauts instead.

Joining in the pre-release media hype, Bantam Books made the unusual move of publishing its movie tie-in version of Tom Wolfe's book two months in advance of opening day, instead of graciously waiting until afterwards. Stuart Applebaum of Bantam told *The New York Times* they were shipping 650,000 copies of the "Now a major motion picture!" edition of *The Right Stuff* early "on a hunch that the continuing interest in the space program, the interest sparked by a female astronaut, and the continuing interest in the candidacy of ex-astronaut John Glenn for President means we'll sell a million copies regardless of how the movie does."

The candidacy of John Glenn for President! If the megaproject *The Right Stuff* needed another thrust to launch it into the stratosphere, this certainly seemed to be it. Of course it's true, as Kaufman repeatedly pointed out, that this was one serendipitous publicity coup that could not have possibly been planned in advance.

"When Tom Wolfe began writing, John Glenn was not yet a senator," said Kaufman in October of 1983. "When I began planning the movie three-and-a-half years ago, Glenn was running again for the Senate, not yet a real contender for the Presidency. I never considered the political ramifications."

Even after Glenn stepped into the race for the Democratic Party nomination for President, Kaufman discounted his chances against Ted Kennedy. But when Kennedy withdrew from the race on December 1, 1982, Kaufman finally realized that he had a hot potato on his hands.

Forget about the effects of Glenn's candidacy on *The Right Stuff*'s publicity and vice versa; with traces of Watergate still lingering in his memory, Kaufman was worried about the effects of Glenn's candidacy on the physical safety of his film. So he ordered that the original negatives be locked away and duplicates be made of all the editors' work prints "just for protection." In case this might be thought of as paranoid, consider that not long after, a 9,000-foot work print that contained the entire Glenn flight disappeared from Kaufman's workshop!

Aside from all the promotional hoopla that surrounded it, the debut of *The Right Stuff* proved to be a magnificent achievement indeed. It was very long—three hours, eleven minutes—but so absorbing and exhilarating you wished it could go on forever. Perhaps the most amazing thing about it was that it managed to translate Tom Wolfe's unique literary style into a credible visual equivalent. Like Wolfe's writing, it sometimes went too far in some directions, getting out of hand as it was straining for effect, but even its shortcomings were exciting.

The critics, being critics, found things to object to, but by and large, they acknowledged Kaufman's stunning feat, with such comments as "*The Right Stuff* ... is probably the brightest and the best rookie/cadet movie ever made, though the rookies and cadets are seasoned pilots and officers. The film almost makes one glad to be alive," praised Vincent Canby in *The New York Times*.

"*The Right Stuff*, which many people thought could never be turned into a movie, is about to splash down in the nation's theaters. And despite a glitch here, a malfunction there, a triumphant landing it is likely to be. . . . Moviegoers seeking a grand yet edifying entertainment, right-stuffed with what Kaufman calls 'seriousness of subject matter and a wild humor that comes out of left field,' now know where to look," wrote Richard Schickel in *Time*.

"Ultimately what makes *The Right Stuff* so stirring isn't the astounding physical feats these heroes perform but the blossoming of their quirky, hard-won humanity. When Gordo ascends the heavens, for example, one is moved not so much by the unimaginable vision he sees but by his face reacting to it. This is one epic as full of soul as it is of spectacle," stated David Ansen in *Newsweek*.

Dennis Quaid came through with particularly flying colors. "I especially liked Dennis Quaid as the cocky, mischievous Gordo Cooper," raved Rex Reed in the *New York Post*.

"Kaufman was extremely fortunate in finding ... Dennis Quaid, who could capture the innocent braggadocio and sublime (but not misplaced) self-confidence of Gordon Cooper," stated Schickel.

"If there's a scene-stealing role it's Dennis Quaid's Gordo Cooper—a man so untroubled, and so uncomplex, that he could fall asleep in the space capsule just before his historic flight," asserted Ansen.

And Pauline Kael of *The New Yorker* commented, "I felt my face twitching, as if I were about to laugh, whenever Dennis Quaid's Gordo was on the screen, because he has a devilish kid's smile, with his upper lip a straight line across his face. ... When he gets his turn in the heavens—Cooper makes the last solo flight into space—his split-faced grin is perhaps the standout image of the film. He's cynical and cocky—a materialist in every thought and feeling—and so when his face tells us that he's awed by what he sees, we're awed by what we see in his face."

The feeling of awe quickly turned to one of shock, however. The meager receipts at the box office indicated that something was going very wrong for *The Right Stuff,* which had ended up costing $27 million. Opening weekend pulled in a scant $1,601,167 in 229 theaters across the country. "*The Right Stuff* is attracting an over-thirty crowd, which is not the audience that goes to the movies," offered a representative for Warner Brothers, the studio releasing the film. To broaden its appeal, they intended to buy advertising time on "youth radio" in selected cities.

A week later, the film was managing to stay alive, but it certainly wasn't breaking any records. Shell-shocked executives tried to pinpoint the mines. "We made a mistake in following the lead of the press," said coproducer Robert Chartoff in *The New York Times.*

"The press picked the movie up as a political polemic. We thought that any kind of publicity space was good space. Now we think certain segments of the public are going to the movie because they think it's a *responsibility*—not a fun movie."

123

"Nobody's interested in a history lesson," summed up another Hollywood executive.

Even representatives of rival studios told the *Times* they were upset over the *The Right Stuff*'s blowout. "What's happening to our industry?" lamented Irv Ivers, a vice-president at MGM-UA. "Throw a piece of garbage out there, and people flock to it."

"There's got to be more to the industry than making a series of *Porky's*," said Lloyd Leipzig, vice-president of publicity at Orion. "The industry usually thrills at another studio's failure. We should support an important picture like *The Right Stuff* any way we can."

Nobody was more stunned by *The Right Stuff*'s commercial failure than its director. "Before it was released, everybody said it was going to make a hundred million dollars," Kaufman mused. By early March of 1984, it hadn't even recouped its production costs, selling barely $20 million worth of tickets.

But there was still a faint hope that the film might pull itself out of its black hole by scooping up a significant number of the eight Academy Awards for which it had been nominated, including Best Picture. As it turned out, *The Right Stuff* slunk away with only four relatively minor awards: Best Film Editing, Best Original Score, Best Sound, and Best Sound Effects Editing.

In a final obituary for the movie in August 1984, *New York Times* entertainment reporter

Aljean Harmetz was now calling the debacle "*The Right Stuff* syndrome," as if a new disease had been diagnosed in Hollywood. "Hollywood's marketing executives . . . are being extra cautious about keeping their movies from getting tangled up with politics," Harmetz wrote.

"The consensus in Hollywood is that *The Right Stuff* got into trouble partly because the movie became inextricably tied to John Glenn's campaign for the Democratic nomination for President and was perceived more as a documentary than as a rousing piece of entertainment."

Harmetz also quoted Warner Brothers advertising vice-president Rob Friedman: "Everyone will always take into account what happened with *The Right Stuff*. The lesson is that people's primary focus when they go to the movies is entertainment."

Dennis Quaid learned a different kind of lesson. "As an artist, you want to reach the widest audience," he said. "But I learned my lesson with *The Right Stuff* because I thought it was going to be the hugest thing that hit the universe. After that I tried not to think about that. I try to have a good time while I'm doing it. That's the only control I have over something."

• 11 •

IF THE RIGHT STUFF COULD BE CLASSIFIED AS SCIENCE *fact*, Quaid's next two projects—*Dreamscape* and *Enemy Mine*—were solid science *fiction*. Although with a little imagination, you might agree with *Dreamscape*'s producer that the idea of a person entering someone else's dream has practical potential.

"It is possible," Bruce Cohn Curtis stated. "It *could* happen in, perhaps, fifty years, because there are dream-research centers operating today. In fact, Joe [Ruben, the director] and Dennis Quaid visited one at UCLA. We also hired a psychic as a technical advisor."

Dreamscape was the baby of Bruce Curtis, scion of one of Hollywood's oldest dynasties. His grandfather Jack Cohn cofounded Columbia Pictures, where his granduncle Harry Cohn served as chief executive for many years. In addition, Curtis's mother worked as a television and stage actress, and his father had a hand in developing the classic On The Waterfront.

Bruce, one could say, had connections. But his family wanted to make sure he worked his way up the Columbia ladder step by step, starting out with the mailroom. He didn't stay on for the full haul; instead, he forged out on his own as an independent producer of such films as Otley, Roller Boogie, Hell Night, and The Seduction.

It was Joseph Ruben—director of Gorp and Our Winning Season—who originally discovered the Dreamscape script in 1981. It just so happened that the agency representing him, William Morris, also handled Dreamscape writer David Loughery, a young television writer who had recently arrived in Hollywood on the heels of winning a scriptwriting contest sponsored by Columbia Pictures while he was a student at the University of Iowa.

Ruben took the Dreamscape script to Curtis— with whom he had worked on the teen crime film Joyride—who just happened to be looking for a project to launch his newly formed Zupnik/ Curtis Productions. Curtis liked what he read, because it was a science-fiction fantasy rooted in the here and now. He was also eager for

a shot at doing a special-effects movie for the
first time.

Curtis gave the go-ahead for a rewrite; the
original Loughery script calling for the virtually total destruction of New York was a little
too rich for any cost-conscious producer's blood,
and a menacing rat-man figure that loomed up
in a couple of dreams was a bit too much of a
cliché.

"We changed that because so much had been
done with werewolves," explained associate producer Chuck Russell. "This was right after The
Howling and An American Werewolf in London
and we felt the difference between a man with
a rat's face and a man with a wolf's face would
be minimal. We wanted to take a different approach. . . . Joe Ruben wanted to go with something that scared him, and since he's scared of
snakes, we went in that direction."

Dreamscape is about particularly potent psy-
chics who can enter other people's dreams,
participate in them, alter them, and even kill
the dreamers, in their dreams—something that's
enough to frighten the victims to real death.

There's the bad guy—a covert-operations
man named Bob Blair (Christopher Plummer),
intent on using psychic dream-linking to kill
the President (Eddie Albert). Then there's the
good guy, Alex Gardner (Quaid), a reluctant
participant in the dream-research project who's
just as intent on stopping Blair's evil machina-
tions.

Along the way, there are some nifty dream sequences that were achieved by using some very tricky and complex special effects. The final scenes, depicting the President's post-nuclear-holocaust dream, were especially difficult. They were set partly in a cramped, murky cave, where the cinematographer hoped to attain greater visual depth by pumping in smoke to diffuse the lighting. Whenever the director was ready for a take, the cinematography crew would blast the grotto full of hot, oily smoke, then wait for the right density while cast and crew stifled chokes behind their respirators.

Then there was the problem of the mutant dogs who attack Quaid in the dream. How to get them to look sufficiently revolting? The special-makeup-effects crew came up with a solution they were mighty proud of: doberman costumes described by the head special-makeup man, Craig Reardon, as "beautiful," with "entrails bulging out of the body and exposed rib cages and boils and french-fried skin."

But the dogs had no respect for their costumes. They trekked around in the muddy cave until their suits got caked with slime. What's worse, the star doberman refused to attack. Instead of lunging at Quaid in the climactic scene, the dog approached Dennis at a trot, and then tried to shake off his costume. The hapless handler defended his dog's professional honor and laid the blame squarely on the costume.

"Reardon sniped parts of the costume's legs

away," *Cinefantastique* magazine reported, "hoping to make it more comfortable, but this produced no better reaction. Next, the dog's owners took to furiously waving a little furry target at the dog, then quickly sticking it just inside Quaid's shirt while everyone enthusiastically urged the dog to attack.

"This made the dog think everyone just wanted to play. It would run up to Quaid, half-hop once, then bark excitedly while waiting for his trainers to get the toy again.

"Quipped Reardon, 'Bruce Cohn Curtis said the mutant dog looked like someone's dirty laundry running across the floor.' Finally the dog made one decent leap past Quaid and Ruben called it a take. The shot is still in the film, although the rest of the mutant dogs were replaced with German shepherds with their fur shaved in patches and dabbled with red goo."

Quaid also had to endure the assault of makeup artists who needed to take a cast of his head with his eyes open in order to fashion his horrific Snakeman head for the movie's final scene.

But when all was said and done, producer Curtis was ecstatic. "I previewed the picture three times and hearing the reaction from the audience is wonderful," he said.

Most of the critics were also gratified, with some reservations, although as usual none of their quibbles related to Dennis Quaid.

"*Dreamscape* works, maybe because it has a

sense of humor," said Roger Ebert, who gave it three stars. "The movie stars Dennis Quaid, that open-faced specialist in crafty sincerity. . . . *Dreamscape* places its characters in a fantastical situation, and then lets them behave naturally, and with a certain wit. Dennis Quaid is especially good at that; his face lends itself to a grin, and he is a hero without ever being self-consciously heroic."

Pauline Kael of *The New Yorker*, who's liked just about everything Quaid has done, said that *Dreamscape* is "an efficient, clever thriller in happy control." Quaid, she wrote, "plays smart here as convincingly as he played dumb in *All Night Long*, and he does it without the element of moral ambivalence that he used as Gordo Cooper in *The Right Stuff*. Quaid combines braininess with a physical ease; he's completely unapologetic about playing a smart character, and he manages to suggest that Alex is capable of putting his brains to use. Quaid plays intelligence and intuition as a sexy advantage."

The difficulties of making *Dreamscape* were like child's play compared with the hardships of *Enemy Mine*. The end result of *Enemy Mine* also showed that investing big bucks and elaborate special effects in a project by no means guarantees a successful end product.

When *Enemy Mine* bowed on December 20, 1985, *Variety* reported that it opened to one

favorable review (from the New York Post's
Archer Winston), and eight unfavorable ones.

Enemy Mine is "a costly, awful-looking
science-fiction epic with one of the weirdest
story lines ever to hit the screen," said Janet
Maslin of The New York Times. "That a lot of
trouble obviously went into the making of Enemy Mine does not make it any more likable."

But who was to know? Enemy Mine was
based on an award-winning novella by sci-fi
writer Barry Longyear. It came to the attention
of producer Stephen (All of Me, Slap Shot, The
Last Picture Show) Friedman when, looking for
a project, he sent an associate to a sci-fi convention in Texas. He was impressed enough to
buy the tale of an earthly starfighter who becomes stranded on a hostile planet with an
enemy alien, and sign on Ed (Ladyhawke)
Khmara as the scriptwriter. Then director Richard Loncraine was hired, although executive
producer Stanley O'Toole did admit that he
was a "strange choice." His credits included
the bizarre Sting vehicle Brimstone and Trea-
cle, and The Missionary, starring Monty Py-
thon's Michael Palin in a biting satire of Ed-
wardian morality.

Loncraine's initial input into the script re-
writes was invaluable, but major problems soon
developed. Actually, Loncraine and O'Toole
philosophically parted company over the choice
of shooting locations even before production
began.

Loncraine's preferred site to represent Fyrine IV—the harsh, mythical planet where most of *Enemy Mine* takes place—was a small island off the coast of Iceland. O'Toole, with his eye on the bottom line, felt that this was ridiculous; Iceland was cold, remote, and very expensive. He had scouted out Lanzarote, in the Canary Islands, as the perfect location.

But off to Iceland they went. "The living conditions were terrible," Hunt Downs, the film's publicity director, said. "We were stuck on an island in the middle of nowhere." Social life consisted of one disco in the village where fights broke out between the locals and the crew over the attentions of the native female attractions.

With such drawbacks, at least the cinematography should have been fantastic. To O'Toole, however, the bleak, grey landscape of Iceland produced footage that "looked as if it was done in a coal mine in England." To make matters worse, the unstable weather—in one day it could go from being foggy to sunny to snowy and rainy and then back again—set the production schedule far behind.

It wasn't long before 20th Century Fox went shopping for a new director. The man they had their heart set on was Wolfgang Petersen, a German director with an international reputation largely stemming from his two previous productions, *Das Boot* and *The Neverending Story*.

Although Petersen was still tied up in post-production work for the American version of *The Neverending Story*, his agent called him at night with an urgent summons; the studio was begging him to read the script. He did, and loved it. For him, *Enemy Mine* was a perfect blend of sci-fi action and an intimate, emotional story between two characters—a sort of cross between Ingmar Bergman and *Star Wars*.

"It's not really a sci-fi picture," he explained. "When I read it, I was thrilled by its unusual quality. A hermaphrodite alien who gives birth and who, in spite of his reptilian appearance, is a complex being. And a young fighter pilot who dares to explore someone so very different from himself and discover what's behind the scaly shell . . . this film calls for peace and tolerance and coexistence—unlike *Rambo*, which is aggressive."

There were several more weeks of negotiations with Petersen—shooting, meanwhile, continued in Iceland before Fox finally pulled the plug on the original *Enemy Mine* in May of 1984. It was, *Starlog* magazine pointed out, "a dramatic move to make once a studio has dumped so much money into a film."

Petersen had agreed to helm a second attempt at *Enemy Mine* under the proviso that he have ample time to prepare it his way. He looked at the dailies that had been shot in Iceland and agreed with O'Toole that the barren Iceland locations did not show up to interesting advantage. Nor was he pleased with very much else about the original—from the set designs to the production crew to some of the cast.

He was given six months for preparation and a free hand in restructuring the project. Basically, he was starting from scratch. He hired a new production crew headed by people with whom he had worked on his other movies. Then he recast nearly all the roles, with the exception of the two top-billed stars. "I had the freedom to recast the film," Petersen said. "But after seeing Dennis Quaid and Lou Gossett in other movies and meeting them personally, I said they're perfect for this film."

It was an arrangement that suited Gossett just fine; he and Quaid were kept on full salary until production resumed in November, and Gossett told columnist Marilyn Beck that he had bought a home with the money he earned not making Enemy Mine.

The next thing Petersen had to do was find a unique, striking location to replace Iceland for the planet of Fyrine IV. O'Toole made another pitch for Lanzarote, and this time the director agreed. "Lanzarote," described the film's production notes, "is an island five hundred miles off the coast of West Africa with a swath of desolate landscape created by three hundred volcanoes, some of which are still active. Deadly eruptions in 1730 and 1824 created the 'aboriginal, spectacular, and frightening' look Wolfgang Petersen envisioned for Fyrine IV."

Only ten days of shooting were actually done in Lanzarote itself. After that, the crew packed up twenty tons of Lanzarote lava rock and hauled it back to Munich, Germany, where it was used to help duplicate the look of the island in model sets constructed on soundstages at the Bavaria Studios.

With the participation of Oscar-winning production designer Rolf Zehetbauer and associates, *Enemy Mine* took over seven of the nine stages at Bavaria, where lavish exterior and interior sets were created—including, according to the production notes, "an aluminum-glittering conception of a wholly computerized manned space station orbiting a distant star system in the year 2085. Visionary details of the station are complete down to easy-chair soda fountains and issues of *Playboy* from the year 2085," and an "operating theater for robot surgery equipped with real Siemens instruments."

Stage 9 at Bavaria, which when completed had the distinction of being Europe's largest, was constructed especially for *Enemy Mine*. It was there that the massive exteriors of the forbidding two-sun, six-moon, glacier-and-petrified-forest-covered planet Fyrine IV were represented.

The sweeping *Enemy Mine* script required such extensive locales. The story is set a hundred years hence, in a distant sun system that is the site of a fierce battle between Earthmen and an alien race, the Drac. When the fighting stops, the only two warriors left are Davidge, the Earthman played by Quaid, and Drac Jeriba Shigan, played by Lou Gossett, stranded on Fyrine IV, an inhospitable place of carnivorous plants and deadly meteor storms. It's not the kind of place where you'd want to get marooned with your best friend, let alone an enemy Drac—who looked like "a combination of a lizard, a kangaroo, a bird, a dog, and a little bit of Stevie Wonder," according to Gossett. Then again, the earthling looked a little strange to the Drac, too.

But the only hope of survival for either of them in this hostile environment is mutual co-operation. Reluctantly at first, Quaid starts making friendly overtures to the Drac and discovers that he's not such a bad guy after all, especially after he stops gurgling and learns a little English. Jeriba, actually the intelligent inheritor of an ancient culture, also starts accepting Quaid, and they team up to protect themselves against the assaults of Fyrine IV.

An unexpected complication arises when Jeriba, who turns out to be a hermaphrodite, impregnates himself and dies in childbirth. The baby Drac becomes Quaid's ward, and much of the rest of the film is spent with Quaid teaching the young Drac how to survive, play football, and evade sadistic earth scavengers who want to capture the Dracling as slave labor for their mine. When they succeed in their nefarious ways, it's up to Quaid to rescue his alien charge.

The technical requirements of this script were truly daunting. There was the look of the Drac, which went through about eight incarnations, ending up, according to the makeup artist, James Cummins, looking "reptilian and dinosaurlike with spikes . . . like a big, ugly hornytoad."

Gossett had to undergo two to three hours of makeup application daily for his transformation into the Drac. Petersen felt it was extremely important that the Drac be believable. "The danger," he said, "was in feeling that there was a man behind the mask, so we designed makeup that enabled Lou Gossett to act, not just walk around with a strange face. He conveys the full range of emotions."

The texture of the mask and makeup Gossett wore had to be very thin in order to let that full range of emotions come through, which is why each day's head had to be scrapped and reapplied in exact duplicate the next day.

That was tough, but small potatoes compared to some of the insults poor Dennis Quaid had to endure over on Stage 9. As Petersen said, "To create a horrible, unearthly ice storm on a stage with falling trees and meteorite showers and monsoonlike rain and fire on the water is very tough, very difficult."

During one sequence, Quaid had to set a lake on fire, with liquid fuel, while standing on a cliff during a fierce storm. All this during the frigid, bone-chilling temperatures of a grey Munich winter that permeated the soundstage.

"Petersen shot this massive sequence on Stage 9 from thirty different angles," *Enemy Mine's* production notes added. "Quaid proved his physical 'cool' during those thirty takes, which required him to stand under drenching ice water, pouring down at a torrential one thousand gallons a minute. Between shots he steamed under the hot lights, wrapped in an electric blanket to get some warmth back into his body."

"This is the biggest, most satisfying role I have ever had," Dennis was quoted as saying about this $24 million epic. "Davidge is a human being who gets to show a lot of sides to himself, and really evolve in the course of the film. There's everything: humor, anguish, tears, hate, pride, love, pain, action. There's no end of action, and I tried to do most of it myself. So it was also physically a very grueling experience."

Grueling indeed!

· 12 ·

WITH THE SHOOTING OF *ENEMY MINE* MERCIFULLY
concluded, Dennis found himself back state-
side in a condition that was very foreign to
him: singlehood. He had been married for five
years to P.J. Soles and had lived with Lea
Thompson for another four. A steady relationship had always been a part of his life, yet
now, for the first time in almost a decade, the
only females in his life were Maggie and Jessie—
his faithful basset hound and golden retriever.

Anyone worrying about Dennis's social life,
however, should have discerned his modus oper-
andi. For a hardworking guy like him, with
little time to himself, the most efficient system
had been to combine business with pleasure. He
met P.J. during *Our Winning Season*, romanced

Lea through *Jaws 3-D*, and then . . . hooked up with Meg Ryan in *Innerspace*.

With bobbed blonde curls framing hazel eyes, Ryan's picture could be the dictionary illustration for the word "cute"; alternately, it could appear next to "perky." At twenty-six, she's ready to pick up where Goldie Hawn left off.

In some ways, Ryan might seem like an East Coast Dennis Quaid—an all-American type and, at the same time, a free spirit who, like Quaid, had quit college midstream to go into acting. While she has committed herself to her chosen career, it is not impossible to imagine her happily going off in a hundred other directions if fate so beckoned. And, like Dennis, her parents were divorced when she was in her teens.

Also in common with Quaid, Ryan has—what else?—the grin. *Rolling Stone* writer Fred Schruers quoted director Peter Hyams's description that "if a normal smile takes a tenth of a second, hers takes longer, and everything in her face changes. People sit in dailies, and when she smiles, everybody goes, 'Ahhh.' "

Ryan grew up in suburban Fairfield, Connecticut, the child of a former regional theater actress and casting agent who taught public school, as did her father. "I was the do-gooder achiever type," Ryan recalled. Following in the footsteps of her journalist stepfather, she began studying journalism at New York University. Then, however, her mother managed to get her an agent who arranged an audition in Los Angeles for the ten-line role of Candice Bergen's rebellious daughter in the 1981 flick, *Rich and Famous*. Not only was it Ryan's first shot at professional acting, it was her first time on a plane. But she still copped the role.

After that followed commercials, small parts on the daytime soap operas *Ryan's Hope* and *Guiding Light*, a role as the high school tramp in *Amityville 3-D* (another rarity she has in common with Dennis (*Jaws 3-D*) Quaid), and then, in 1983, a featured role as Betsy Montgomery on the CBS soap *As the World Turns*.

"Sometimes," Meg said about Betsy—who immortalized the line, "Love is big"—"I just want to break out of character and say, 'Don't let yourself be battered around by events, don't be totally male-defined, don't be so vulnerable.' " Clearly, the real-life Meg was a lot more together than the soapy Betsy.

After two years with *As the World Turns*, Ryan headed to Los Angeles for a role in the short-lived Disney comedy-Western series *Wildside*, and stayed on to make movies. First she played the wife of the doomed pilot Goose (Anthony Edwards) in *Top Gun*, a role that expanded into an offscreen relationship as well. Then came *Armed and Dangerous*, a zany comedy with John Candy and Eugene Levy.

Innerspace was next. In this comedy/fantasy/thriller directed by Joe (*Gremlins*) Dante and

143

"presented" by Steven Spielberg, Ryan plays Lydia Maxwell, a pert reporter in love with the rogue test pilot, Lieutenant Tuck Pendleton (Quaid)—a guy who's fond of looking in the mirror and proclaiming, "The Tuck Pendleton machine. Zero defects."

Tuck's got a goodly dose of sexy magnetism, but his drunken episodes and adolescent behavior finally get to be too much for Lydia and she walks out on him shortly before he is to undergo his most daring mission ever: He and his space capsule are to be miniaturized and injected into a rabbit.

Only instead of the rabbit, Quaid's host for his fantastic voyage winds up being a weird, hypochondriac supermarket clerk named Jack Putter (Martin Short). Together they share drinks, dancing, and indigestion in some hilariously inventive scenes that earned the movie the 1987 Academy Award for Best Visual Effects. Then, with Quaid's air supply running low and lots of people trying to sabotage everything, Ryan teams up with Short in the race to extract Quaid and re-enlarge him in time.

Sort of silly, but lots of fun. Especially for the cast. Because most of Short and Quaid's scenes together were ones in which they talk to each other without being in the same shot, they used headsets to communicate. Dennis was placed in a soundproof booth while Short would hear him over a little speaker, but their dialogue was recorded simultaneously. Comic timing was crucial.

So the guys did what any regular cutups would—they did their best to crack each other up. "He does a very good Jerry Lewis, and I would do Dean Martin, and we were Martin and Lewis for about five weeks," reported Dennis. "Then I was John Wayne and he was Katie Hepburn for a while. This bar at the hotel every Thursday night had lip synch, and we'd do Dean and Jerry doing 'I've Got You Under My Skin.'"

And for the most part, their ploys worked. At least as far as the critics were concerned. Roger Ebert called *Innerspace* "an absurd, unwieldy, overplotted movie that is nevertheless entertaining. . . . The performances are so engaging and the effects are so enthusiastic that even though the movie runs long, it's only because it has too many ideas."

"The movie jumps all over the place, without obeying any rules. Still, *Innerspace* is consistently funny. . . . It makes the Rhine journey down the gullet every bit as exciting as a voyage to Saturn," said *New York* magazine.

As always, Quaid's performance garnered high praise, and the critics did not fail to notice Ryan's engaging performance, either. Pauline Kael of *The New Yorker*, for instance, praised her "blitheness," which "gives the picture a lift; she brings a quirky, resilient spirit to the scenes in which she and Short have to chase after the thieves in order to locate the tiresome microchip and save Quaid."

No one was more surprised by this positive response to *Innerspace* than Quaid, who thought of the movie as a good silly comedy that the critics would hate. It was one of the few times in his career that he didn't even do any research for a part; he was going to wing it through this one for the sheer fun of it.

The producers had taken the project very seriously, however—if $27 million in production costs is any indication. And nobody was more surprised than these producers when the huge audiences they anticipated for *Innerspace* never materialized. Just as *The Big Easy* had been a surprise success of the season, *Innerspace* was a startling failure. Released in the summer of 1987, it had only rung up $13.7 million in domestic box-office rentals by the end of the year, ranking it number thirty-seven, according to the *Variety Show Business Annual* for 1987.

In hindsight, this failure was attributed to a flawed marketing campaign. "They made it look like a space hardware adventure instead of a human comedy," Quaid told Roger Ebert. The last word is that the studio is planning to rerelease the film with a new advertising approach.

Still, for Meg Ryan, her high profile and good critical notices in *Innerspace* marked a professional watershed. It taught her, she explained, "the word *no*. I can actually afford to wait for something that really excites me."

Personally, she did not have to wait long for excitement; she found it right on the set of *Innerspace*—in the form of Dennis Quaid. They've been an item ever since, and as the months go by, they've gotten bolder about proclaiming their relationship in public.

Although Dennis was down in Louisiana filming *Everybody's All-American* on the day Meg turned twenty-six, he wasn't a bit shy about sending his birthday greetings. He actually hired a high school marching band, decked out in full tricolor regalia, to accost Ryan on the Paramount set where she was shooting her upcoming film, with a booming version of "Happy Birthday to You" and a banner that announced: "HAPPY BIRTHDAY MEG, I LOVE YOU! . . . . . DENNIS!"

Ryan, for her part, said, "Talk about passion for life! [Dennis] has such a great sense of humor." As red-hot as he may be in the public eye, she added, "He's as normal as they get—unpretentious, with great charm."

It's a scenario with definite possibilities, although neither party is rushing things just yet. Ryan shares her Santa Monica digs with a fellow actress and has said, "I think I may be independent to a fault." She also remarked, "I don't see the white picket fence and the kids for a while. I just can't imagine getting married and starting a family. I couldn't handle all the details."

Following *Innerspace*—where Meg and Dennis's scenes together were severely limited by the fact that, as she explained, "There were very few moments when he's not five inches tall and inside Martin Short's intestines"—the two would hitch up for more evenly proportioned costarring turns in *D.O.A.*

Then Ryan lit off on her own again to make *Promised Land*, released in February of 1988. She plays a tough, trashy drifter in this dark story based on a real-life incident involving two former high school classmates in a small Idaho town whose divergent paths reunite in a tragic final shootout.

Her other recent shoots included *Presidio*, costarring Sean Connery as her authoritarian father and Mark Harmon as her lover.

Since Ryan has said she never really thought of herself as sexy, she researched her role in *Presidio* by interviewing others about what turns them on in a woman. Along the way, she probably also gathered some insights for the original screenplay she has been cowriting called *Between Engagements*, about a girl who never quite manages to make it through the "I do's."

"I'm the B+ person pedaling twice as fast as everyone else," Ryan said, summing herself up. That's not what Dennis has said, however. As he told *Elle*, "Meg is extremely smart and very versatile. I think she'll be one of our best actresses. She's very choosy about what she does. She's smarter than I was."

* * *

After *Innerspace*, Dennis moved on to the terrific *The Big Easy* and the not-as-terrific *Suspect*. But no matter what his role happens to be, his reviews have just kept getting better.

New York magazine critic David Denby called Quaid's appearance in *Suspect* his "most self-assured performance yet. His hair is longer and fuller than before, and he's all but dropped the rakish grin that was so likably cocky in *The Right Stuff* and *The Big Easy*. For the first time, he seems like a grown-up man—a complex man, with dark, even malevolent corners as well as plentiful charm."

Quaid plays Eddie Sanger in *Suspect*, a slick, morally ambiguous dairy-industry lobbyist on Capitol Hill who finds himself as one of the jurors in a murder case being handled by somber Washington, D.C. public defender Kathleen Riley, played by Cher. Smitten with Cher, Quaid brazenly flouts the lawyer/juror connection taboo and helps her clear her client by discovering clues that point to the real murderer.

As for their connection on the set—well, the inimitable Cher described it like this to *People* magazine: "He was like Kurt [Russell, her *Silkwood* costar], this annoying little pest. But he was so cute. He'd annoy the s--- out of me, then flash that smile. I had to laugh. We had one bedroom scene in *Suspect*. I was nervous, and he kept busting my chops. I told him, 'Hey, Scum [that was her pet name for him], I wish I had known you were such a sex symbol."

Cher also said that she really liked the script even though she felt intimidated by all the lawyerly material expected of her. "To play the lawyer, I had to learn to say a lot of complicated legal things as if I understood them," she told Roger Ebert. To get a better feel for her role, Cher spent considerable time in the company of real Washington, D.C. public defenders, following them on their rounds of courts and jails.

It's no surprise that the research-obsessed Quaid spent a month in D.C. before filming, boning up on everything about his lobbyist character, down to the approved "power" ties and lace-up shoe styles.

"They had me in Beverly Hills, Rodeo Drive kind of shoes when I came," Quaid explained. "But one of the most important things about researching a character is the shoes—how they make you feel. I find I can walk more like a lobbyist in lace-ups."

He also, *New York Times* reporter Barbara Gamarekian wrote, "hung about Capitol Hill receptions, committee hearings, and bill mark-ups, [and] found a political mentor in Gaylord Nelson, the former Democratic senator from Wisconsin, who now works for the Wilderness Society here.

" 'Dennis came out to our place for dinner, and we talked about lobbyists and what they do, and I read the script and gave them some advice on technical points on legislative procedure,' said Mr. Nelson."

Executives at Tri-Star were brimming with confidence in the $14 million film, directed by Peter Yates. Preview audiences had been enthusiastic, and Tri-Star decided to go for a wide initial distribution. But like many producers' best-laid plans, this one fizzled at the box office when it opened in late October 1987.

The failure of Suspect was more a fault of the storyline than the actors, many critics said. David Ansen in Newsweek, for example, wrote that "Suspect, an entertaining but implausible courtroom thriller directed by Peter Yates, has the good fortune to have Cher and Dennis Quaid as its stars. Her pugnacious, earthy charm and his playful self-confidence delightfully divert the audience from the script's glaring contrivances."

Of course, nobody has ever said that the path to leading-man stardom was strewn with surefire hits. Another small pothole along that road has been Quaid's most recent starring vehicle, D.O.A., a remake of the 1949 B-movie classic that featured Edmund O'Brien as a businessman who's been poisoned and has forty-eight hours to discover who his killer is.

In the hands of stylish young producers Rocky Morton and Annabel Jankel, inventors of that computerized hipster Max Headroom, Quaid's D.O.A. sounded promising. "Having done Max

Headroom, we didn't really want to do another film that was so dependent on technique," Jankel explained. "We were interested in storytelling."

Quaid's character is updated to a college English professor and one-time successful novelist whose life has stalled with a bad case of writer's block. His wife wants to divorce him because of it, and his colleagues resent him because of it—even though he hasn't published anything in years, he's still got the cushy tenured professorship he landed back when he was a literary boy wonder. In fact, someone is disturbed enough by this beleaguered professor to slip him a slow-acting but deadly mickey.

The premise is still an interesting one, especially helped along by Meg Ryan to give it some extra verve as a college student who's stuck on her English professor—both figuratively and literally, when Quaid superglues her arm to him to make sure she comes along to help investigate his murder.

But Dennis, whose thirty-four-year-old head of hair had to be shaved into an exaggerated widow's peak to simulate the forty-year-old character he plays, knew it was a risky undertaking. "It's a stretch—it's a real stretch," he said. "I might fall flat on my face. It's also one of the most enjoyable things I've ever done. . . . It's either going to be one of the worst or one of the best things I've ever done."

Quaid, as always, turned in a rock-solid performance. As New York Times critic Caryn James said in her review, he's "an actor with the spark and intelligence to carry off just about anything."

But the overly stylized movie was all over the place and no place at once; it never really came together. James called it "one of the season's biggest disappointments." Meg Ryan, she said, "matches Mr. Quaid's ability to make third-rate dialogue sound better than it is, but even they can't make this sound better than second-rate."

Roger Ebert liked it better, calling it "a witty and literate thriller, with a lot of irony to cut the violence. Quaid is convincing as the chain-smoking English professor, Meg Ryan is true-blue as the stalwart coed."

After an initial flurry of interest in the film when it opened on March 18, 1988, audiences seemed to side with the James camp. In an April 6, 1988, box-office roundup, *Variety* reported that by its third weekend, *D.O.A.* "dredged up an unthrilling $1,443,613 in 869 stations ($1,661 per) for a 43 percent drop. With a seventeen-day take of $10,020,391, pic seems destined to be Buena Vista's [the distributing arm of The Walt Disney Company that handled *D.O.A.*] first underachiever in about a dozen releases."

No sympathy cards were necessary for Quaid, however. This is, after all, a man who put the Hollywood roller-coaster ride in healthy per-

spective a long time ago. As he said in *Elle*,
"Chasing the box office is a crock of shit. That's
not real. What's real is when you're actually
doing the work. That's the only time I have
control over what I do. After that, it's up to
advertising departments, trends, and people's
taste."

▪ 13 ▪

BUT LET'S SUPPOSE FOR ONE SECOND THAT SOME misguided Hollywood bigwig, on the basis of D.O.A., pronounced Dennis Quaid to be box-office poison. In other words, what if Quaid's acting career ended today? What in the world would he do?

For Dennis, a more appropriate question would be: What would he do first? Which of his myriad interests would he next pursue with the enormous energy he's put into his acting?

Would it be his music? Always an avid singer/songwriter, Dennis's musical passion has been whipped up even more by the heady experience of recording his composition "Closer to You" for the *Big Easy* record album, in the company of such New Orleans musical institutions as the Neville Brothers.

He has been saying for a long time that he'd like to take a year off, cut an album, and perhaps go on the road touring. As a step in that direction, he's formed a band recently called the Eclectics ("It's not Dennis Quaid and the Eclectics," he insisted modestly to *Rolling Stone*, "it's Dennis Quaid *of* the Eclectics"), and they're in the process of negotiating a record deal.

On Christmas Eve of 1987, Dennis and his band performed one of his original compositions—"(Homeless) Frame of Mind"—at a dinner for 4,000 homeless people (and a few socially conscious stars) at the Convention Center in Washington, D.C. He awakened to the plight of the homeless while making *Suspect*, which involves a homeless Vietnam vet unjustly accused of murder.

If all goes well with his record deal and an Eclectic tour materializes, down-home Dennis has also said he'd rather sharpen the act in small clubs than shoot for "the Roxy right off or have my own TV special."

Then again, might we hear Quaid's gravelly baritone wafting into the cabin of a 747 one day, declaring, "Ladies and gentlemen, this is your captain speaking . . ."? His love for flying, developed during *The Right Stuff*, has never abated, and he still explores the wild blue yonder every chance he gets in the single-engine planes he is licensed to fly.

Or maybe Dennis would go back to baseball if his film career ended, verifying a statement in one of his earliest publicity releases that "Dennis admits that if he had not become an actor, he would have been a ballplayer." Although he is probably a little over the pitcher's mound for that by now.

The point is, however, that dedicated as Quaid is to his acting craft, Hollywood is by no means the be-all and end-all of his existence. A few years ago, his ex-wife P.J. Soles described Dennis as having "a very strong, secure feeling about himself and a great faith in the film industry, but he doesn't take it overly seriously. He could have been a gas-station attendant and still be happy."

With over two dozen movies and stage productions under his belt, the same holds true today. Dennis has been knocked about hard enough by the unpredictable vicissitudes of show business—including shocks like the box-office failures of *The Right Stuff* and *Innerspace*—to know what's real and what's just glitter.

He enjoys, for instance, his black BMW and his new home in the Hollywood Hills—decorated in a playful funk style that includes a 1956 Wurlitzer jukebox in the kitchen and some goofy Wild West bedroom furniture with wagon wheels for legs.

But what's really real to Dennis is his ranch in Montana. It's just a stone's throw from his old, unfinished Montana dream house, the one he has since claimed was an albatross around his neck; the one he sold in 1983 when he decided to work for himself instead of a house.

His newer spread—1,400 acres of wilderness adjacent to a national forest—used to belong to director Sam Peckinpah and Quaid's *Tough Enough* costar, the late Warren Oates. Quaid and Oates had become good friends, and Dennis appreciates knowing that there's still something of Oates around; his bones were spread around a campfire on the property after he died.

Dennis recently attended the intimate wedding of actor Kiefer Sutherland, son of actor Donald; he goes trout fishing with actor Chris Lemmon, son of Jack; and he plays golf with musician pal Bob Seger.

But Dennis's two most faithful companions are his ever-present dogs, Maggie and Jessie. He even takes them to his movie sets to remind him of home. Family is important to him, too. Dennis's new Los Angeles house is very close to Randy's, and he also makes sure to spend time with his twelve-year-old stepbrother, Buddy.

Of course, no matter what other interests Quaid might pursue, there's no danger of his acting career ending today. Or tomorrow. Or anytime in the foreseeable future. He's too much in demand—by his fans and by movie producers, those perceptive animals who know a hot thing when it's been sizzling in front of them long enough.

Early 1988 found him in the middle of shooting *Everybody's All-American*, directed by Taylor (*An Officer and a Gentleman*) Hackford and costarring Jessica Lange. Quaid plays a former Washington Redskins star halfback who's flabby and washed-up at forty-seven. It's taken Dennis a lot of marathon pasta sessions to try to make that one look realistic.

He's also gone through another physical battering, as if he hadn't had enough of that in films like *Tough Enough* and *Enemy Mine*. In order to recreate one particular moment of his character's old NFL glory in *Everybody's All-American*, Quaid had to make his own end run rather than rely on a stunt double, because his helmet is knocked off and the audience can see his face.

Quaid gamely donned his uniform—including an old-fashioned, underpadded helmet like they used to wear in 1969—and went out onto the field so he could get knocked out of bounds by linebacker Tim Fox, former All-Pro safety for the New England Patriots.

Dennis is no fool; he had a good idea what he was in for. Just before shooting began in Louisiana State's Tiger Stadium one evening, he said to entertainment writer Gene Siskel, "I'm really going to get hit."

On the first take, Fox pronounced that Dennis "took a real good hit that time." The helmet flew off as planned, but director Hackford was not satisfied. He felt that Dennis had slowed down near the sideline, like he knew what to expect. "I'm giving it all I've got," Dennis protested.

But then he realized he could give it just a little bit more. For take two, he decided, he would turn his body into the hit. That would do it. And it did. It broke his collarbone.

Siskel reported that Quaid had a stunned audience of about 100 crew members and 1,800 extras watching from the bleachers as he lay writhing in pain on the field. Like a real pro, though, he was up in less than two minutes and joking with Hackford: "Hey, Taylor, I want bump money! I want bump money!"

About all he did get was a brace he was instructed to wear for six weeks, and an excuse from shooting the few remaining football scenes.

Meanwhile, simmering on the burner is another Quaid project, *Great Balls of Fire*, the story of hot rocker Jerry Lee Lewis, slated for filming under the direction of Jim (*The Big Easy*) McBride.

Terrence Malick, of *Days of Heaven* fame, wrote the script based on a book by one of Lewis's ex-wives, and though Mickey Rourke was reportedly first considered for the role, it's a good thing the producers came to their senses. Can you think of a better choice than Quaid to play the original wild and crazy rock 'n' roller?

Way back in *The Night the Lights Went Out in Georgia*, Travis/Dennis groped for a way to explain his popularity as a performer. "I have a wildness that people like," he concluded. Add a touch of the grin, a pinch of the bad-boy charm, a dash of the rippling abs, and you've got a Quaidian recipe for success that'll do The Killer proud.

It should also keep Dennis's popularity smoldering for a long, long time.

FILMOGRAPHY

I NEVER PROMISED YOU A ROSE GARDEN
(1977, New World Pictures)
Costars: Kathleen Quinlan
                                        Bibi Andersson
Director: Anthony Page
Producer: Roger Corman

SEPTEMBER 30, 1955
(1978, Universal)
Costars: Richard Thomas
                                        Susan Tyrrell
                                        Dennis Christopher
                                        Thomas Hulce
Director: James Bridges
Producer: Jerry Weintraub

OUR WINNING SEASON
(1978, AIP)
Costars: Scott Jacoby
                  Deborah Benson
Director: Joe Ruben
Producers: Joe Roth, Lou Arkoff

BREAKING AWAY
(1979, 20th Century Fox)
Costars: Dennis Christopher
                  Daniel Stern
                  Jackie Earle Haley
Director: Peter Yates
Producer: Peter Yates

GORP
(1980, Filmways)
Costars: Michael Lembeck
                  Philip Casnoff
Director: Joe Ruben
Producer: Jeffrey Konvitz

THE LONG RIDERS
(1980, United Artists)
Costars: Stacy & James Keach
                  David, Keith &
                     Robert Carradine
                  Randy Quaid
                  Christopher & Nicholas Guest
Director: Walter Hill
Producer: Tim Zinnemann

ALL NIGHT LONG
(1981, Universal)

Costars: Barbra Streisand
                    Gene Hackman
Director: Jean-Claude Tramont
Producers: Leonard Goldberg,
                      Jerry Weintraub

CAVEMAN
(1981, United Artists)
Costars: Ringo Starr
                    Barbara Bach
Director: Carl Gottleib
Producer: Turman/Foster Productions

THE NIGHT THE LIGHTS WENT OUT IN GEORGIA
(1981, Avco Embassy)
Costars: Kristy McNichol
                    Mark Hamill
Director: Ronald F. Maxwell
Producers: William & Carole Blake

BILL (TV film)
(1981, CBS)
Costars: Mickey Rooney
Director: Anthony Page
Producer: Alan Landsburg

JOHNNY BELINDA (TV film)
(1982, CBS)
Costars: Rosanna Arquette
                    Richard Thomas
Director: Anthony Page
Producer: Lorimar/Stonehenge

TOUGH ENOUGH
(1983, 20th Century Fox)

Costars: Stan Shaw
                         Warren Oates
Director: Richard Fleisher
Producer: Bill Gilmore

JAWS 3-D
(1983, Alan Landsburg Prods.)
Costars: Bess Armstrong
                         Louis Gossett, Jr.
Director: Joe Alves
Producer: Rupert Hitzig

THE RIGHT STUFF
(1983, The Ladd Co.)
Costars: Sam Shepard
                         Ed Harris
                         Barbara Hershey
                         Scott Glenn
Director: Philip Kaufman
Producers: Chartoff/Winkler

BILL: ON HIS OWN (TV film)
(1983, CBS)
Costar: Mickey Rooney
Director: Anthony Page
Producer: Alan Landsburg

DREAMSCAPE
(1984, 20th Century Fox)
Costars: Max Von Sydow
                         Kate Capshaw
                         Christopher Plummer
                         Eddie Albert
Director: Joe Ruben
Producer: Bruce Cohn Curtis

ENEMY MINE
(1985, 20th Century Fox)
Costar:	Louis Gossett, Jr.
Director:	Wolfgang Petersen
Producer:	Stephen Friedman

INNERSPACE
(1987, Warner Bros.)
Costars:	Martin Short
	Meg Ryan
	Kevin McCarthy
Director:	Joe Dante
Producer:	Michael Finnell

THE BIG EASY
(1987, Columbia)
Costars:	Ellen Barkin
	Ned Beatty
Director:	Jim McBride
Producer:	Stephen Friedman

SUSPECT
(1987, Tri-Star)
Costars:	Cher
	Liam Neeson
	Joseph Mantegna
	Philip Bosco
Director:	Peter Yates
Producer:	Daniel A. Sherkow

D.O.A.
(1988, Touchstone)
Costars:	Meg Ryan
	Charlotte Rampling
	Daniel Stern

Directors: Rocky Morton, Annabel Jankel
Producers: Ian Sander, Laura Ziskin

EVERYBODY'S ALL-AMERICAN
(upcoming, Warner Bros.)
Costars: Jessica Lange
       Timothy Hutton
Director: Taylor Hackford
Producer: Stuart Benjamin

ABOUT THE AUTHOR

GAIL BIRNBAUM is a New York-based writer whose work has appeared in such publications as *People*, New York *Daily News Magazine*, *Savvy*, and *Women's World*.

She is currently writing a screenplay about Woodstock and the summer of '69; it's too early to tell whether Dennis Quaid will star.